ICFA Continuing Education
Managing Currency Risk

Proceedings of the AIMR seminar *Managing Currency Risks for Investment Portfolios and European Monetary Union: Changes and Opportunities*

April 8–9, 1997
Zurich, Switzerland

Jon R. Bailie
Jean-Pierre Beguelin
Paul Burik
Paul Day
Mark P. Kritzman, CFA
Stefan Laternser
Ronald Layard-Liesching
Mark Lundin
Robert C.J. Meijer
Patrizio Merciai, *Moderator*
Patrick Odier, *Moderator*
Richard B. Olsen
Bruno Solnik
John C. Stannard, CFA
Ram Willner
Daniel R. Witschi

To obtain the *AIMR Publications Catalog,* contact:
AIMR, P.O. Box 3668, Charlottesville, Virginia 22903, U.S.A.
Phone 804-980-3668; Fax 804-980-9755; E-mail info@aimr.org
or
visit AIMR's World Wide Web site at **www.aimr.org**
to view the AIMR publications list.

ISBN 1-879087-96-0
Printed in the United States of America
November 1997

Editorial Staff

Terence E. Burns, CFA
Vice President

Charlene Semer
Editor

Jaynee M. Dudley
Production Manager

Roger Mitchell
Assistant Editor

Lois A. Carrier
Typesetting/Layout

Contents

Foreword

Currency risk is the inevitable byproduct of global diversification of portfolios. For investors who are relatively new to the international arena, currency risk is a monster to be feared and isolated. The presentations in this proceedings show that it can be understood and tamed. Indeed, it can even be profitable.

Managers will always face certain hard-core decisions with respect to currency risk—for example, whether to hedge, and if so, how much and with what instrument(s); whether to evaluate currency risk in isolation or along with asset risk as part of the total risk package a particular foreign investment entails; whether return should be denominated in the base currency or the foreign currency; and if these decisions seem too difficult or time-consuming, whether to use a currency overlay manager. Authors of presentations in this proceedings address all of these issues, and more.

Among the particularly current and particularly intriguing questions addressed in this proceedings is what will happen to European markets if monetary union comes to pass in January 1999. The U.S. and Japanese bond and equity markets will no longer dwarf the European markets; the new euro markets will be huge. Presumably, currency risk will disappear from intra-European investments because all assets will have to be denominated in the common currency (the euro) and because separate exchange rates will no longer exist. Instead, country risk will dominate the investment decision; the EMU will not directly affect the political policies of member countries, although establishment of the European Central Bank will further encourage more-unified monetary policies and greater price stability. Can monetary unity work at all if some large-market, EMU-resistant European countries (e.g., the United Kingdom and Denmark) fail to participate and others cannot meet the convergence criteria by 1999? The discussion of the EMU in this proceedings will be of vital interest to managers who are invested in some European countries now and will soon find themselves invested in Europe as a whole.

We hope this proceedings will help readers better understand currency risk. The presentations are accompanied by a reference list, which should prove useful to readers wishing to explore specific aspects of currency risk more closely. We extend special appreciation to Patrizio Merciai and Patrick Odier, both from Lombard Odier & Cie, for their valuable contributions as moderators of the seminar. We also wish to thank the authors of these presentations: Paul Day, Quorum Capital Management; Mark P. Kritzman, CFA, Windham Capital Management; Stefan Laternser, Bank Julius Baer; Ronald Layard-Liesching, Pareto Partners; Mark Lundin, Olsen & Associates; Bruno Solnik, HEC School of Management; John C. Stannard, CFA, Frank Russell Company; and Ram Willner, Pacific Investment Management Company.

Katrina F. Sherrerd, CFA
Senior Vice President
Educational Products

Biographies

Paul Day is an investment analyst at Quorum Capital Management Limited. Previously, he was a tutor and lecturer in mathematics at Lady Margaret Hall, Oxford University. Mr. Day holds an M.A. from Cambridge University and a Ph.D. in mathematics from Oxford University.

Mark P. Kritzman, CFA, is managing partner of Windham Capital Management. Prior to joining Windham, he held investment positions at The Equitable Companies, AT&T, and Bankers Trust Company. Mr. Kritzman serves on the prize committee of the Institute of Quantitative Research in Finance, the review board of the Research Foundation of the Institute of Chartered Financial Analysts, and the editorial boards of the *Journal of Derivatives* and the *Financial Analysts Journal*. He has published numerous articles in academic and professional journals and is the co-author of the *Dictionary of Financial Risk Management* with Gary Gastineau; *Currency Management: Concepts and Practices* with Roger Clark; and *The Portable Financial Analyst*, *Asset Allocation for Institutional Portfolios*, and *Quantitative Methods for Financial Analysis* with Stephen Brown. Mr. Kritzman holds a B.S. degree from St. John's University and an M.B.A. from New York University.

Stefan Laternser is vice president and head of bond research with Bank Julius Baer & Company, Limited, Zurich. Previously, he served as senior bond manager for the Bank in Liechtenstein; bond analyst and portfolio manager with Vontobel Asset Management; equity analyst and project manager for Swiss Volksbank, Zurich; and accountant with Laternser Treuhand. Mr. Laternser holds a Ph.D. in modern finance and an M.A. in auditing and trust from the University of St.-Gallen (HSG).

Ronald Layard-Liesching, a founding partner and director of research at Pareto Partners, is responsible for ongoing research and product development. Formerly, he was director of quantitative products for County NatWest Investment Management and managing director of Chase Investment Bank. Mr. Layard-Liesching has more than 20 years of experience in quantitative modeling and currency management and has written and lectured extensively on risk-management techniques. Mr. Layard-Liesching holds a B.A. in mathematics and economics from Lancaster University.

Mark Lundin is a research scientist at Olsen & Associates. He holds a B.S. in mathematics and computer science from the University of Illinois and a Ph.D. in high-energy particle physics from the University Louis Pasteur in Strasbourg, France.

Patrizio Merciai is executive vice president in charge of investment strategy for Lombard Odier & Cie. He is an associate professor of economics and banking at the University of Geneva and has served as consultant to several multinational companies. Professor Merciai holds a doctorate in political science from the Graduate Institute of International Studies in Geneva, Switzerland.

Patrick Odier is managing partner at Lombard Odier & Cie. He is president of the foundation board of the International Center for Financial Asset Management and Engineering, vice president of the board of the Swiss Banking School, and current president of the Executive Committee of the International Finance and Commodities Institute. Mr. Odier holds a degree in economics from the University of Geneva and an M.B.A. from the University of Chicago.

Bruno Solnik is professor of finance and chair of the Finance and Economics Department at the HEC School of Management and chair of the finance and economics department. Prior to joining HEC, he served on the faculty of the Stanford Business School and as a visiting professor at the University of California at Berkeley, the University of California at Los Angeles, the University of Strathclyde, and the University of Geneva. Professor Solnik is former president of the European Finance Association; serves on the board of editors of several major finance journals in the United States, Europe, and Asia; and sits on the AIMR Council for Education and Research.

John C. Stannard, CFA, is director of Russell Data Services, a division of Frank Russell Company. In previous positions with Frank Russell, he served in quantitative services, performance measurement, and the consulting group. Mr. Stannard has also held positions as an investment analyst with Barclays and as an assistant portfolio manager. He holds a B.S. in pure mathematics from Royal Holloway College, University of London.

Ram Willner is international market strategist and risk manager for Pacific Investment Management Company and adjunct professor at the University of California at Irvine. Prior to joining Pacific, he served as a fixed-income research analyst with Sanford C. Bernstein & Company and as professor of corporate finance and business administration. Mr. Willner holds a B.A. in mathematics from Brandeis University, an M.B.A. from Carnegie–Mellon University Graduate School of Industrial Administration, and a D.B.A. from Harvard Business School.

Managing Currency Risk: An Overview

Managing currency risk is one of the most important aspects of investment management. For any investor based in any currency, the majority of fixed-income and equity investments lie outside the home country, including the United States and Japan. Thus, the introduction of currency risk is an inevitable consequence of international diversification. The importance of managing currency risk for global stock and bond portfolios cannot be overstated: ineffective currency-risk management can significantly and negatively affect portfolio returns.

Currency-risk management raises important issues for portfolio managers, plan sponsors, and global investors. The hedging decision depends on the investment horizon and the percentage of assets allocated outside the home country. Designing effective hedging strategies requires understanding how correlation affects the minimum-risk hedge ratio; estimating an investor's utility function and degree of risk aversion; and comparing the availability, liquidity, and pricing of alternative hedging instruments. The choice between actively and passively managing currency risk involves analyzing the extent to which active currency management can potentially add value. An investor may use major foreign currencies as a tactical asset but actively manage emerging market currencies. After analyzing the costs and benefits, investors may want to hire a currency overlay manager to manage currency risk. Integrating global asset allocation and currency allocation decisions, another approach to managing currency risk, can produce superior risk-adjusted returns and add more value than other active and passive currency management strategies. Performance attribution analysis decomposes excess portfolio returns into the asset allocation effect, the security selection effect, and the currency effect, providing performance results that are consistent with the investment decision-making process.

Assessing the effects of unprecedented structural changes such as the upcoming European Monetary Union (EMU) is another challenging task for global equity and fixed-income portfolio managers. The prospect of European currency union underscores the importance of credit analysis in European fixed-income research and will be the catalyst for structured product development. Monetary unity will eliminate currency risk among EMU participants—the big negative to investing outside the home country—although currency has been only a modest source of risk for core-country participants. Local currency-risk and -return statistics for select European markets over different time periods indicate that opportunities will remain for active managers to add value through effective country allocation.

This proceedings is the published record of an AIMR seminar intended to give participants an understanding of the important aspects of managing currency risk—a topic of growing importance to global investors. The authors draw on their extensive experience as currency-risk managers to assess changing currency risk, evaluate the decision to hedge or not to hedge, and analyze alternative hedging strategies. They provide an overview of active currency management, an explanation of the role of currency overlay managers, a strategic look at integrating global asset allocation and currency management, and a method for performance attribution. Looking toward the future, as successful portfolio managers do, many of the presentations examine the implications of the EMU for security analysis.

CHANGING CURRENCY RISKS

A significant amount of financial research has focused on forecasting the direction of movements in exchange rates to determine whether they follow a random walk and whether investors can use deviations from the purchasing power parity (PPP) model or the uncovered interest rate parity (UIRP) model to earn excess returns. Ram Willner reviews empirical studies of exchange rate movements under PPP and UIRP conditions, interpreting the results before and after 1990—the turning point at which the forecasting ability of these two models changed significantly. Using a balance-of-payments-crisis model, he assesses the potential for emerging markets—the next frontier for active currency managers—to experience a currency crisis. Willner also addresses the problem of currency contagion.

Standard currency models produce mixed results, depending on the time period studied. Although the pre-1990 evidence indicates that exchange rates fluctuate in a random walk and do not gravitate toward PPP, the evidence after 1990 strongly favors PPP, which is found to have a half-life of three to five years. Thus, PPP is a long-term factor that must be an integral part of any currency-movement analysis. The UIRP approach has virtually no value after 1990, at least not for European currencies. Fundamental changes in market dynamics—including more-favorable secular economic trends, better central bank and government policies, and improved capital mobility—have altered the behavior of currency returns and currency risk. Opportunities in major currencies are now limited to tactical allocations, although strategic opportunities exist in some emerging-market currencies.

Balance-of-payments-crisis models focus on key variables such as government macroeconomic policy, the trade balance, and foreign currency reserves. Portfolio managers can use such models to identify potential emerging-market currency crises. These speculative crises can be averted, however, by governments that are willing to raise interest rates and to impose politically unpopular austerity measures. Investors must also watch out for a currency crisis that is contagious among countries, especially weak countries with strong trade relationships or similar economic policies.

CURRENCY HEDGING

The currency-hedging decision is probably one of the most debated topics in global portfolio management and the focus of extensive financial research. Mark Lundin reviews global investment diversification for risk-reduction purposes and the resulting foreign exchange risk. He compares static with dynamic hedging and provides an overview of the goals and constraints of hedging models. He also presents an algebraic derivation of foreign investment risk variables and the optimal static hedge ratio and demonstrates that minimizing portfolio value at risk does not always mean adopting a systematic full-hedging policy.

Investors seek to reduce portfolio volatility through diversification, particularly among markets that have weak correlations with each other, but global diversification introduces currency risk to a portfolio. Although the effect foreign exchange (FX) risk has on returns depends on the time period analyzed, FX-adjusted volatility increases, on average, by 30 percent compared with domestic-only returns.

Global investors with more than 5–10 percent of their portfolios dedicated to foreign assets must address the problem of managing currency risk. Should they hedge symmetrically or asymmetrically? Should they manage currency risk passively or actively, hedging when returns are unfavorable and lifting the hedge when returns are favorable? The major difference between static hedging and dynamic hedging involves a trade-off between adaptability to market changes and transaction costs. Static hedging is less adaptive to changes in market conditions and is relatively inexpensive; dynamic hedging is more adaptive and involves higher transaction costs. Hedging also has a *threshold effect*; that is, investors have a marginal propensity to hedge—the greater the portfolio value at risk, the more investors are willing to pay for complicated hedging strategies.

Successful FX trading models consistently generate high performance with small capital drawdowns by analyzing FX movements and generating explicit, real-time trading recommendations that a human trader can execute. They warn of potential deals a few minutes in advance, do not frequently change recommendations, and support stop-loss around the clock.

The global static hedging ratio is simply –1 times the correlation between the underlying investments and FX fluctuations multiplied by the ratio of standard deviations of the underlying investment and the FX itself. Dynamic hedging involves changing the hedge ratio to one that is optimal at any given time. It can incorporate desired rules for the hedge ratio and investors' constraints. Efficient frontiers for dynamic currency overlays illustrate that optimizing portfolio value at risk does not necessarily require a hedge ratio of –1 and that if the correlation between the underlying investments and FX equals zero, then FX may provide further diversification benefits and no hedge is recommended.

Once portfolio managers make the decision to hedge, they must carefully analyze all available hedging strategies and instruments. Mark Kritzman explains that the motivation for currency-risk management is to maximize expected utility and notes that institutional investors may define utility in absolute terms, relative terms, or both. Because the relevant correlation is that between foreign asset returns in the investor's base currency and currency returns, the minimum-risk hedge ratio fluctuates. Few foreign portfolios have enough diversification between the currency and the base-currency-denominated assets to make the argument that diversification overcomes the volatility that currency exposure introduces to a portfolio.

Simultaneously maximizing absolute returns on an underlying portfolio and relative returns on a currency benchmark moves global investors from the efficient frontier to the efficient surface. Joint optimization in three dimensions—expected return, volatility, and tracking error—almost always produces better results than constrained mean–variance analysis. Thus, mean–variance tracking-error optimization increases expected return with the same level of standard deviation and tracking error, reduces standard deviation of returns at the same level of return and tracking error, or produces less tracking error at the same level of expected return and standard deviation.

Nonlinear hedging strategies, which generate curved payoff functions, are an effective method for managing currency risk. Nonlinear strategies include traditional currency options, contingent currency options, and hybrid collars, some of which can be difficult and expensive to obtain. Traditional currency options protect a portfolio from downside currency risk below a specified threshold, preserve the potential to experience currency gains, and annually cost about 3–4 percent of the portfolio. Contingent currency options protect a portfolio from currency losses beyond a specified threshold *only* when the portfolio's local return also falls below a specified hurdle value; they cost less than traditional currency options but also provide less protection. A hybrid collar provides protection against concurrent currency losses *and* portfolio losses in exchange for giving up currency gains when the portfolio's local returns exceed a certain threshold. Evaluating the relative performance of nonlinear hedging strategies requires evaluating them against a relevant nonlinear or optionlike benchmark. Value-at-risk analysis is very helpful in determining the cash flow implications of these strategies.

ACTIVE CURRENCY MANAGEMENT

The potential for adding value through active currency management affects the choice between actively and passively managing currency risk. Paul Day explains that simple currency management tools work reasonably well, especially when managers use several models to reduce risk. He discusses how to use and interpret the results of the variance ratio with respect to trending, provides several strategies for exploiting serial correlation in currency returns, and reviews the downside risks inherent in active currency management tools.

To be successful, active managers need credible processes that are robust, not period specific and not dependent on outliers to identify trends and to take advantage of the forward rate bias. Over the 1978–97 period, when the forward premium has been positive (negative) and when foreign interest rates have been lower (higher) than domestic interest rates, currency returns have been negative (positive). Thus, active management of currency, using convex payoff models or technical strategies, can enhance portfolio returns, but these strategies have downside risk.

The variance ratio summarizes trend information over a particular horizon. It is a useful first step in analyzing potential currency trends, but it can be period specific. Although the variance ratio applied to the DEM/USD rate over the 1975–97 period implies that some trend exists, the ratio would not identify a general upward trend with continual fluctuations around it. Other models are available for identifying serial correlation, and not all of them are entirely independent. Classes of models include convex payoff models that involve option replication and dynamic hedging; statistical time-series models; and well-known technical-trading rules, including moving-average methods, filter rules, and gapping. The weaknesses of these models include unknown forward volatility, unstable parameters, and false signals, all of which increase the downside risk of getting whipsawed by the market.

Historical experience indicates that a currency overlay program, over the long term, can add an additional 1–2 percent in annual return after fees. Ronald Layard-Liesching warns that fund managers must realize the *episodic* nature of hedging return opportunities before implementing a currency overlay program. He provides an overview of currency overlay programs, reviews hedging and accounting issues, outlines alternative currency overlay strategies, and explains how to implement an effective currency overlay program.

Currency hedging is never intended to increase the existing currency-risk level but, rather, should focus on systematically reducing pre-existing, unmanaged price exposure. Hedging losses are cash losses, whereas currency translation gains are unrealized paper gains. Furthermore, because currency overlay is a hedging activity, the returns from an overlay program must be viewed together with the underlying currency translation gains or losses on global investments.

The different philosophies of currency overlay management are reflected in the objectives of alternative overlay strategies and the return payoffs they offer. Forecast-based approaches primarily focus on achieving returns, and risk-controlling currency overlay styles focus on avoiding currency losses relative to a benchmark. A successful forecast-based style can provide substantially higher returns than a risk-controlling approach in the short run, but returns can be substantially negative and volatile in the longer term, which suggests that clients should compare the long-term performance of alternative styles.

Implementing an effective currency overlay program requires clearly specifying whether the goal for the program is protecting assets or enhancing return. The overlay manager operates independently from the underlying global equity and bond managers and needs to know only their currency allocations and which instruments they hold. The overlay manager evaluates performance relative to an unhedged benchmark on a monthly basis and charges fees based on performance or portfolio size.

ASSET ALLOCATION AND CURRENCY MANAGEMENT

Differentiating between hedged and unhedged returns in the short run and the long run and understanding currency's contribution to total portfolio risk are helpful in confronting the problem of currency risk in portfolio management. The long-run difference in return between hedging and not hedging global equities and bonds is only about 1 percentage point. Over the short run, however, currency makes a significant, but marginal, contribution to stock returns and a very large contribution to bond returns. Bruno Solnik provides an overview of currency risk. He explains how strategic currency allocation involves determining the appropriate currency allocation in the passive benchmark, compares alternative strategies for currency allocation, and presents a tactical currency allocation model designed to achieve excess returns.

Strategic currency allocation involves deciding on the appropriate currency allocation in the passive benchmark (to measure performance and guide long-term investment) and determining the approach to managing currency risk—an integrated approach or a separate currency overlay manager. Integrating global asset allocation and currency allocation decisions, using *joint optimization*, produces the highest risk-adjusted returns and value added—especially for bonds—relative to partial and separate optimization through a currency overlay manager.

Although the currency market is efficient, currency risk premiums fluctuate over time because of business cycles, changes in the market environment, central bank interventions, and changes in investors' relative degrees of risk aversion. Thus, the optimal currency-hedging policy will vary considerably over time because the sign and magnitude of the risk premium on each currency are likely to change. Using tactical asset allocation and allowing for the separation of market and currency selection, the optimal hedging strategy outperforms both full-hedging and no-hedging strategies, but evaluating its effectiveness requires many years.

PERFORMANCE ATTRIBUTION

Analyzing a portfolio manager's success in the context of the investment decision-making process is the main objective of performance attribution. John Stannard provides the basic framework for performance attribution, giving single and multicurrency examples of how the theory is applied in practice and evaluating the basic rules of attribution.

Performance attribution is an acid test for portfolio managers and a valuable business management tool, providing feedback between portfolio managers and clients. An effective performance attribution framework is consistent with the decision-making process, accurately reflects investors' objectives, and identifies both superior performance and areas for improvement. Focusing on the big picture to get a broad sense of how well asset classes have performed is the best starting point for performance attribution.

A single-currency framework decomposes sources of return into the index contribution, the asset allocation effect, and the security selection effect. Examining how the portfolio has performed in particular markets relative to the policy benchmark determines the opportunity cost or benefit of not investing at the benchmark. Multicurrency attribution takes into account the results of physical exposures in non-base-currency markets plus the impact of currency hedging via forward contracts. The traditional currency effect is further decomposed into the forward premium effect (reflecting the effects of relative interest rates and currency premiums) and the currency management effect—which takes into account the management of currency movements over and above those explained by forward premiums.

An effective benchmark defines the natural position of an investment strategy and is best described as an independent hurdle rate that objectively tests the strategy's effectiveness. Thus, the choice of a global benchmark is an important decision, given the different construction methodologies of available benchmarks. In practice, multilevel analysis addresses strategic performance questions, relating results back to original decisions made within the investment process.

LOOKING TOWARD THE FUTURE

The coming European Monetary Union will change the landscape of fixed-income and equity markets throughout Europe. The introduction of a common currency will present significant challenges and opportunities for portfolio managers and investors.

The EMU will create a huge bond market—about USD7.6 trillion as of 1996, or about 37 percent of the world bond market—and will drastically change how global fixed-income analysts and portfolio managers conduct business and create value. Stefan Laternser provides an overview of the new euro market and new strategies that will replace traditional European fixed-income strategies. He estimates the impact of the EMU on credit ratings and credit spreads of the new euro issues, emphasizes the primary importance of credit-risk analysis, and discusses the increasing importance of managing instrument risk and prepayment risk as a structured product market develops in Europe.

The loss of 14 currencies and 14 yield curves in the post-EMU period will reduce traditional fixed-income strategies to a pure interest rate strategy for euro portfolios, combining changing portfolio duration and creating exposure to different segments of the yield curve. Other strategies that will evolve include vertical diversification into lower quality credits, horizontal expansion into emerging market sovereign risk in hard-currency markets or newly emerging currency markets, and a focus on option and prepayment risk instruments to enhance total returns.

As EMU participants lose their sovereign risk status and their right to service debt in a non-EMU currency, bond analysts, portfolio managers, and investors will focus more attention on credit-risk analysis and sovereign-risk management. New ratings philosophies differ for new euro debt issues, but the euro market will be initially rated, on average, Aa1/AA+. Thus, some companies could have higher credit ratings than the countries in which they are located. Post-EMU credit spreads could range from 0–10 basis points for France and Germany to 40–80 basis points for Italy.

New segments of the European bond market will develop as a result of monetary union, including structured products and corporate investment-grade, high-yield, and distressed securities. Structured products, by permitting the "engineering" of credit risk and transfer of prepayment risk, can solve a lot of problems facing international banks and can clean up their balance sheets. Evaluating structured product opportunities for risky investors will require extra homework to analyze the collateral, structure, tools, and the instrument itself. Fixed-income analysis in the post-EMU era will require a traditional economic background, a strong accounting background, and a mathematical or theoretical background to effectively analyze sovereign risk, credit risk, and instrument risk.

CONCLUSION

Even after the advent of the EMU, currency-risk management will remain one of the most important tasks of global portfolio managers because of its significant effect on risk and return in the short run. In this proceedings, the authors bring together an important blend of experience, skills, and foresight to help readers understand the nature of currency risk, quantify its effect, and design effective strategies to manage it. For readers interested in further reading on managing currency risk, a reference list is included at the end of the proceedings.

Changing Currency Risks

Ram Willner
International Market Strategist and Risk Manager
Pacific Investment Management Company

Do currency returns follow a random walk or can a 10 percent undervaluation of the Big Mac in one country lead to a 3.5 percent appreciation in the currency over the following year? Standard currency models—purchasing power parity and uncovered interest rate parity—provide mixed results depending on the time period studied. Although major currencies should be a tactical asset rather than a strategic asset, emerging market currencies are the next frontier for active currency managers despite increasing risk of currency contagion.

A significant amount of research has been devoted to forecasting the direction of movements in exchange rates. Economists use standard economic models to forecast movements in exchange rates, and these models have been tested time and again to analyze whether exchange rates follow a random walk, whether opportunities exist for investors to profit from exchange rate deviations from the purchasing power parity model, and whether the uncovered interest rate parity model can be used to profit from investing in currencies of countries with high interest rates relative to other countries. These models produce interesting results depending on the time period analyzed.

This presentation reviews empirical studies of exchange rate movements under both purchasing power parity and uncovered interest rate parity conditions, interprets the results before and after 1990 (the turning point at which the forecasting ability of these two models changed significantly), offers explanations of what happened in 1990, and discusses investment implications for the post-1990 period. In addition, a balance-of-payments-crisis model assesses the potential for emerging markets—the next frontier for active currency managers—to experience a currency crisis. The concept of currency contagion addresses the idea that if one country experiences a currency crisis, other countries with strong trade relationships or similar macroeconomic policies will also experience a currency crisis.

CURRENCY MODELS

Two of the standard models that are used to analyze exchange rates and exchange rate movements are purchasing power parity and uncovered interest rate parity.

Purchasing Power Parity

The theory underlying purchasing power parity (PPP) asserts that if a good is easily traded in different markets, it should effectively sell for the same price in all of those markets; that is, exchange rates should simply be a translation of one price into another price. For example, if a Big Mac is USD2.00 in the United States and DEM4.00 in Germany, the exchange rate should be two German marks per U.S. dollar according to PPP, because the product is the same in both countries. Economists feel good about this concept because it makes sense, characterizing the nominal exchange rate as the real exchange rate times the relative price levels of two countries.

Initial evidence, at least prior to 1990, indicates that exchange rates fluctuate in a random walk and do not gravitate toward PPP. Thus, investors could actually make money by investing in the high-yield currency or a currency on which the interest rate is high. Such a currency should depreciate quickly, but history shows that this effect does not always happen.

Trending, along with other anomalies, is evident before 1990, although currencies are not supposed to have trends. Nothing is supposed to trend in capital markets, because people would not want to sell (buy) at the current price an asset that will increase (decrease) in price. They would always want to sell or buy at the expected future price.

■ *PPP evidence prior to 1990.* Richard Roll (1979) showed that real exchange rates essentially follow a random walk. Remember that real exchange rates should revert to their PPP value, but Roll found they did not. Meese and Rogoff (1983) used three different PPP models to try to predict the direction of currency movements. Using linear models, they studied pre-1979 currency changes in an attempt to predict them from 1979 to 1983. But they used 1979–83 inputs in their model, which gave the model a better chance of predicting the direction of currency movements using PPP as a relevant factor. Even so, they could not find PPP to be a determining factor in their equations. When they varied the coefficients, the model still did not work. Again, PPP, which makes sense in every economist's gut and should work, did not work.

Bilson (1984) adapted PPP for use in predicting currency movements. His paper was somewhat controversial and was much debated in terms of transaction costs and the technology he applied. Again, PPP did not hold up very well, at least not in the literature.

PPP evidence after 1990. The articles after 1990 virtually all say that PPP does have an effect on exchange rates. Froot, Kim, and Rogoff (1995), for example, concluded that currency movements are not a random walk, because PPP has an effect. The difference, and the reason this effect was not caught before, is that the effect is long term. Consensus estimates the half-life of deviations from PPP at about four years for exchange rates among major industrialized countries. This finding is important in modeling currencies, because models should include a long-run PPP effect.

Throop (1993) showed that PPP used as a factor in currency-prediction models improves errors by 30–45 percent, again at a long run of four to eight quarters. Mark (1995) showed that PPP is not only statistically significant but is also economically significant.

Cumby (1993) wrote an amusing article in which he used the McDonald's Big Mac as a fairly common good throughout the world. A 10 percent undervaluation of the Big Mac led to a 3.5 percent appreciation of the currency over the following year. Again, these results were statistically significant. The *Economist* every year lists Big Mac prices and how close they are to PPP; they are not that close, although many people argue that Big Macs are different in different countries.

To summarize, the evidence after 1990 strongly favors PPP. The PPP effect has a half-life of three to five years and is thus not a trading strategy, but it is a long-term factor that should be included in any currency-movement analysis.

Uncovered Interest Rate Parity

The uncovered interest rate parity (UIRP) concept says that the appreciation or depreciation of a currency against another currency is a function of relative interest rates in the two countries. Think of the process as simple arbitrage. For example, I borrow in one currency, translate it into U.S. dollars, and invest the U.S. dollars at a higher interest rate. I owe a net currency at a lower short rate, but I gain in the United States at a higher short rate. The differential of those two interest rates should be compensated for by appreciation or depreciation of the relevant currency. Otherwise, I have borrowed for nothing and have some sort of capital gain at the end, which is an arbitrage opportunity.

UIRP evidence prior to 1990. Because of the depreciation or appreciation of currency relative to the interest rate differential, currency investment in countries with high yields is profitable. If a currency has a high yield relative to, say, the U.S. dollar, it should depreciate. Think of the interest rate as a discount factor; discounting a currency at a higher rate means the future value of the currency is lower. Arbitrage opportunities will not exist if UIRP keeps the differential in line.

Bilson (1981), in his speculative efficiency hypothesis paper, applied a fairly simple test using only nominal interest rates and achieved significant risk-adjusted returns, measured by the Sharpe ratio. Were his results an aberration? Other research has reconfirmed this finding, providing empirical evidence that you could profit by investing in currencies in countries with high real yields. **Figure 1** shows the potential cumulative profits from speculating in currencies on the basis of Bilson's speculative efficiency hypothesis. The upward trend in cumulative profits confirms Bilson's work up until 1990, but since 1990, volatile cumulative profits resemble a random walk.

UIRP evidence after 1990. After 1990, the UIRP approach has virtually no value, at least not with European currencies. Investing in currencies of countries with high real yields—which were not as high as the 1980s—would not be a profitable strategy.

The behavior of spot–forward price differentials in emerging or developing market currencies and in developed or mature market currencies is compared in **Figure 2**. The Czech koruna and the Indonesian rupiah have made significant profits since 1993, appreciating around 1.9 percent and 2.8 percent, respectively, while the British pound and the German mark have hovered around zero.

Interpreting the UIRP evidence. In the 1980s, currencies offered some positive returns, but later returns were uncertain, possibly for the following reasons:

- *Risk premium.* If the gains reflect a risk premium, then risk should be present. UIRP should not

Figure 1. Cumulative Speculative Profits from Currencies before and after 1990

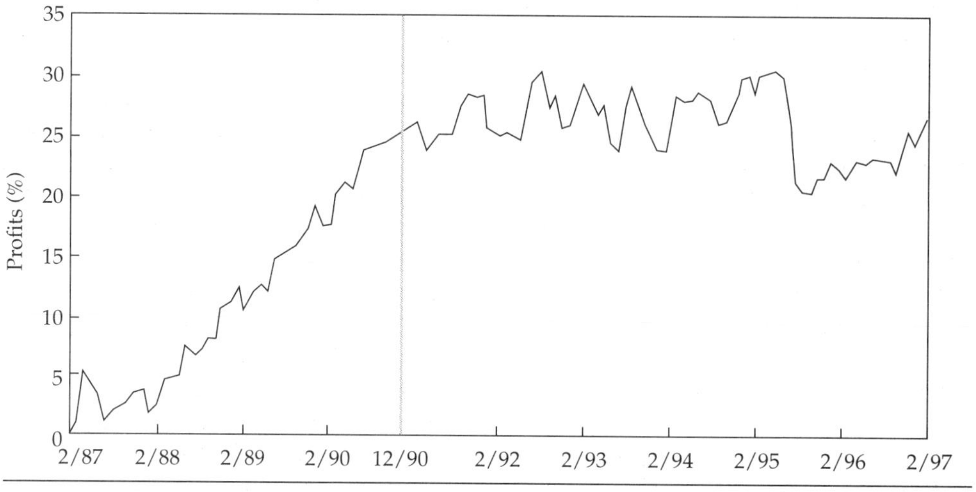

Figure 2. Cumulative Performance for Four Currencies: Realized Spot versus Forward Rates, 1993–97

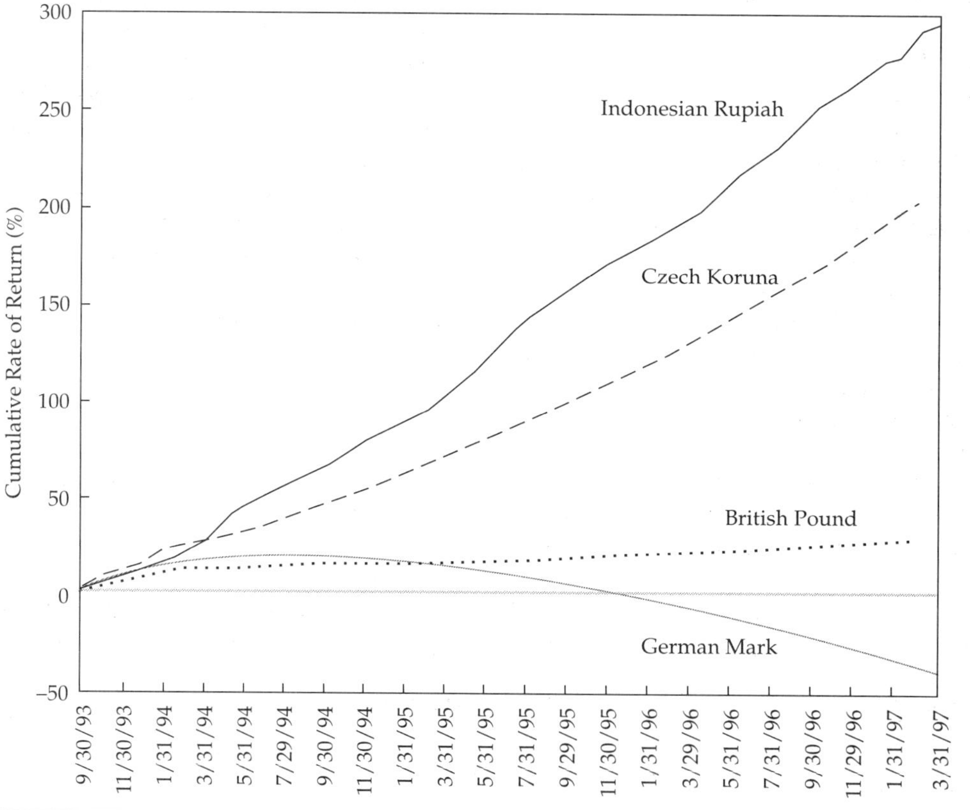

have the effect of sometimes working and sometimes not, although it seems to work. One possibility is that the 1980s were not typical; perhaps in the 1920s, for example, enough declines occurred to justify the risk premium theory. Maybe we are lucky that investing in high-real-yield countries and their currencies has recently worked.

- *Inefficiency.* Another possibility—the one that I like—is the inefficiency story. Most emerging-market investors are domestic. For a U.S. investor in the 1980s, for example, investing in Europe was considered avant garde. Domestic investors do not face diversified situations, but they have to deal with higher volatility than diversified investors, and the risk premium compensates domestic investors for the higher volatility. International investors might be interested in appropriating some of that risk premium for themselves.

- *Growth*. Another story is the growth story: Governments maintain high real yields to keep inflation low, to make sure the economy grows but does not overheat, and to encourage a high savings rate. China, for example, follows such policies. Eventually, this tactic does not work, because foreign investors come in and take advantage of it. But a policy of maintaining high real rates is not necessarily a negative for the currency.
- *Mature currencies*. Perhaps UIRP works only for mature currencies; that is, currencies that are already mature and easily available in general international markets are not going to display the emerging or developing market phenomenon. This effect does not occur for European baskets of developed currencies, but it occurs for emerging market baskets. It worked in Europe in the 1980s, but it no longer works there.

CURRENCY TRENDING

Because currencies seem to trend, trend strategies can make money. Levich and Thomas (1993a) demonstrated that using a simple rule, such as the moving-average rule, can be profitable, as shown in **Table 1**. For example, an investor following a five-day moving-average trading rule buys (sells) the currency if the moving average of a currency's exchange rate for the past five days is above (below) the current exchange rate. The trend-following strategy worked for the 1976–90 period for major currencies—the Canadian dollar, Japanese yen, U.K. pound, German mark, and Swiss franc—producing mean returns of 6.8 percent. Levich and Thomas also examined the performance of a 5-day/20-day moving-average trading rule over the same time period, which produced similar returns of 5.0 percent.

For the same strategies over the 1991–96 period, the returns are negative, –2.1 percent for the 5-day moving average and –1.1 percent for the 5-day/20-day moving average, although they are not statistically significant. Something obviously changed after 1990, because the moving-average strategy produces the same results as PPP and UIRP.

Evidence of currency trending is no longer prevalent, although some trending occurred in the U.S. dollar after 1990 and occurred recently in the yen. In fact, the yen hit a new high against the dollar on April 8, 1997. So, some trending does occur, but not to the same extent as before 1990.

To understand why trending occurs, look at each individual case and focus on the central bank's role. Earlier instances of government intervention have been destabilizing, although the aim was to move the currencies toward PPP equilibrium. More recent central bank interventions (for example, since the Louvre Accord in 1987) have been much more stabilizing and have focused on reducing currency volatility. The profitability for investors in the earlier interventions was fairly good, because it bucked the market trend, but the results for investors have not been quite as clear for the stabilizing interventions.

A series of papers by Lewis (1995) and Kaminsky and Lewis (1996) studied the effects of central bank interventions on exchange rates and developed a clever model. One of the results supposes a currency is moving along at a stable rate when the system suddenly sustains a shock and the currency appreciates. The government tries to resist that change, so rather than the currency moving up directly, the currency appreciates a little. Economic forces push the currency higher, but the government resists that movement, resulting in a trend.

The Kaminsky and Lewis papers focused on government intervention and the creation of trends and found that this kind of phenomenon exists. The government absorbs the currency value loss by engaging in an uneconomical venture—the central bank transfers wealth to speculators, who are betting against its efforts. The government's success in push-

Table 1. Returns on Two Moving-Average Strategies

	1976–1990		1991–1996	
Currency	Strategy I	Strategy II	Strategy I	Strategy II
British pound	7.8%	7.4%	–3.3%	–5.5%
Canadian dollar	2.6	1.0	1.2	3.0
German mark	5.7	11.0	–1.9	–3.3
Japanese yen	2.3	10.9	–4.3	2.7
Swiss franc	6.7	4.0	–2.2	–2.4
Mean	6.8	5.0	–2.1	–1.1

Note: Strategy I — If MA(5) > current value Buy
If MA (5) < current value Sell
Strategy II — If MA(20) > MA(5) Buy
If MA(20) < MA(5) Sell

Source: Levich and Thomas (1993a).

ing or resisting currency value changes is a function of available reserves. For example, Japan has a much greater chance than Chile of successfully manipulating its currency.

WHAT HAPPENED IN 1990?

Evidence clearly suggests that, in the 1990s, we are dealing with a different set of behaviors, a different set of characteristics, and a different set of risks than before 1990. Our ability to analyze currency movements has improved. Advances in technology, not only computing technology but also analytical technology, now include cointegration, variance ratios, error correction, and generalized autoregressive conditional heteroscedasticity (GARCH) models. Having more data also helps.

In addition, secular trends in the 1990s are dramatically different from trends in the 1980s. As bond investors, we have changed our outlook to being long-run bullish because the secular trends are toward a long-term decrease in interest rates. Interest rates have declined dramatically since the 1980s. The United States is currently at a cyclical peak, but rates will be coming down. Exchange rate volatility is also expected to decline.

International capital moves faster now than before 1990. Technology to move capital around and information technology have improved. Bond market vigilantes—speculators or anyone willing to take advantage of an aberration in the market—are a force mitigating all the successful excess profit activity in the markets. Investors quickly take advantage of any disequilibrium or arbitrage opportunities.

Because central banks and governments understand their roles better now, deficits are lower and governments have better control of growth with lower inflation. All these factors tend to stabilize and change the dynamics of currency. Open economies, trade agreements, and other provisions allow currencies to fluctuate in a more natural way. In addition, governments and investors are taking a longer term view.

An important factor is that currencies, at least the western European currencies, have matured, and a whole new set of currencies is maturing now. Good examples of maturing currencies are the Polish zloty and the Czech koruna. On the other side of the world are the Indonesian rupiah and Thai baht. Such currencies are marked by high real yields. Mature currencies are marked by high liquidity, proliferation of associated securities, and lower real yield.

Major currency approaches today should be oriented toward long-term investment rather than short-term trading, although some case-by-case exceptions apply—perhaps the yen is an exception. Key factors to analyze before investing in currencies include the fundamentals of government policy and the capability for enforcement, inflation rates, and the level of foreign currency reserves.

Emerging market currencies aside, currencies are generally a net zero-return investment. Currencies, at least the major currencies, are a tactical asset rather than a strategic asset. If you have a particularly good reason for investing in a currency, invest on a long-term, strategic basis, because no one currency is going to outperform another. In the major currencies, we look for specific macroeconomic policy changes or specific movements associated with the EMU, but the investment decision is more on a tactical basis relative to emerging market currencies.

THE NEXT FRONTIER: EMERGING MARKET CURRENCIES

In the emerging markets, some of the opportunities that were profitable in the 1980s may still be available. Although emerging market currencies have potential value, investing in emerging markets and in emerging market currencies also entails risks.

Balance-of-Payments-Crisis Model

Krugman (1979) developed the basic model that assesses the potential for a currency crisis. The end result of a balance-of-payments crisis is rapid currency depreciation. Krugman's model starts with an overly expansive domestic policy that leads to an overvalued currency and generally a trade imbalance—Mexico is a perfect example. The central bank then draws on reserves to support the currency, which is now generally under speculative attack. Finally, the central bank reaches a crisis level of foreign exchange reserves, and the currency apparently cannot be defended—obviously a situation to avoid.

Even though the Krugman model was developed in 1979, it is still relevant for developing markets because it focuses on the key variables—government macroeconomic policy, the trade balance, and foreign currency reserves—associated with potential emerging market currency crises. Krugman points out that the crisis causes, rather than being caused by, a lack of foreign exchange reserves, because speculators anticipate a decline in reserves. The total exposure of the country matters most, and the potential draw against the currency includes not only outstanding obligations against that currency but also real assets—physical property and corporations are potential draws. Thus, the amount of foreign currency the country must hold is huge, and the central bank has only a small chance of holding off a speculative attack.

For a central bank to successfully thwart a currency crisis requires sufficient currency reserves and a willingness to raise interest rates. A country may have plenty of dollars and thus sufficient reserves, or it may receive a foreign bailout, as Mexico did from the United States. Although actions on the part of the government to raise interest rates and impose other austerity measures are generally politically unpopular, they can successfully stave off a speculative crisis, but the government must have enough character to take these kinds of measures in order to support the currency.

Currency Contagion

One of the reasons for foreign bailout is the problem of currency contagion. The peso devaluation crisis has been labeled the "tequila effect," but countries as distant as Thailand and Indonesia suffer from the same kind of problem that Mexico experienced. Contagion is simply the notion that a currency crisis is contagious—if one country is in a crisis, other currencies will likely experience a crisis. Eichengreen, Rose, and Wyplosz (1996) addressed the issue of currency contagion in emerging market currencies, citing interdependency of trade as the primary cause. A secondary cause is similar macroeconomic policies or fundamentals. Suppose one country's government artificially maintains high employment through its fiscal policy. If that currency suffers a crisis, another country applying the same policy is likely to suffer a crisis also. General investor or speculator nervousness is another possible reason for contagion, because an informational or signaling effect exists. Although nobody wants to cause a speculative crisis, once a currency crisis starts, an onslaught of speculators and investors follows.

For example, in 1992, a currency crisis in the Finnish markka created an advantage for Finland in shared export markets, particularly those shared with Sweden. Sweden started to suffer an imbalance of payments as Finnish goods became more attractive, leading to an anticipated and actual decline in reserves. The Swedish krona then fell, so one crisis led to another crisis—clearly a case of contagion. If you are investing in currencies with countries that have a strong trade relationship, you need to worry about the correlation between the countries.

Sachs, Tornell, and Velasco (1996) looked at the "tequila effect." They found that countries that showed evidence of similar problems were the ones hardest hit. For instance, the countries that were hardest hit had easy credit, overvalued real exchange rates, and particularly low reserves. A country hit by this type of currency contagion usually has poor fundamentals that are similar to those of countries previously hit by a currency crisis.

Eichengreen et al. showed that contagion resulting from trade interaction is statistically significant. In addition, they used probability models to demonstrate that if a currency crisis occurs anywhere in the world, the likelihood, on average, that another country will have a crisis increases by 8 percent, even if the countries have no trade relationship.

The statistical relation between similar macroeconomic policies or fundamentals and currency contagion was much weaker than that for trade relationships, but some evidence supports other causes for currency contagion, especially if the similarities are through several variables rather than only one. Weak countries are also more likely to experience a currency crisis than strong countries, especially countries that are weak in the same respects as the country originally affected by a crisis.

LESSONS

The behavior of currencies has changed dramatically since 1990. Investors cannot apply some of the pre-1990 principles to the post-1990 period, especially in major currencies, although some of those principles might still be true for emerging market currencies. Economists now think that PPP holds in the long run, that UIRP holds in major currencies, and that a trend-following strategy is no longer profitable for most major currencies—Japan is a recent example—although trend following may still be valid in some emerging markets.

Possible reasons for the change since 1990 are more-favorable secular economic trends, better central bank and government policies, and the ease of capital movement. So, fundamental changes in market dynamics have affected the behavior of currency returns and currency risks. Tactical opportunities exist in major currencies, although most of the juice has been squeezed out of them. Strategic opportunities in currency exist primarily in emerging markets. In simple terms, investing in emerging market currencies that have high real yields seems to make money. Trending may work, but investors should also look for long-run PPP effects.

Currency contagion is a significant possibility, and investors should be concerned about it in their analysis of investments. The new rules are not completely clear, so investors should not generalize; they still need to look at conditions on a case-by-case basis. I have suggested where value might be found, although finding it requires work. Tread cautiously, but look closely at the emerging markets.

Question and Answer Session

Ram Willner

Question: Given the new factors affecting currency markets in the 1990s, could there be a run on all currencies at once?

Willner: Theoretically, of course, if a run happened on all the currencies, the result would be mass inflation. Anything is possible, but that development would be highly unlikely. What is more likely is panic and a flight to safety. Such currencies as the Swiss franc, the German mark, and the U.S. dollar might strengthen. Europe could pose some problems, however. We looked at what is going on, because of the potential for inflation as the European countries come into the recovery. The United States is in late-term recovery right now. Because of the potential for some inflation, I am not sure you would see much running to the European currencies, but such an event might happen in a time of severe danger. People would probably call for the gold standard, too. Emerging market investors face a higher possibility of a general run on virtually all of those currencies, as we saw in 1995. Investors must proceed with caution. Emerging markets were extremely profitable in 1996, so those people who remained invested in those markets have recovered well.

Question: Do you view emerging markets, as a whole, as one asset class in which we gradually are making the market more efficient and are using their diversification effects in a better way, or do you see major differences among them according to such features as country fundamentals or stage of development?

Willner: We generally see the emerging markets as an asset class and deal with them as a whole. We prefer this approach partly to get a grip on those kinds of countries but also partly because emerging markets are correlated and they act alike. We look hard at the macroeconomic fundamentals, particularly government policies. For instance, look at Singapore's policies versus Argentina's policies, a comparison that also involves analyzing the political situations. You also have to consider the fundamentals. We examine all of these countries and then find the ones whose fundamentals we like. We like countries that have high real yields but that also try to maintain low inflation. We then segregate the specific group within the emerging markets that we like and invest in those countries. We hold as a group the countries with fundamentals we like, and we do not differentiate among them. Investing in a bunch of the countries that you like in order to get the diversification effect is one of the keys to emerging market investing.

Question: Do you have any recommendations as to which emerging market is the most interesting?

Willner: We are taking a more defensive stance than usual right now. We like some of the better European credits—Poland and the Czech Republic, for example. We are at this point probably staying away from Russia. We also have a position in Argentine currency and paper. We tend to think about the question of investment in bonds and paper as different from the investment in currency, and generally, we hedge currency. If we think the currency is valuable, we do not hedge or even take a currency position. With Argentina, for instance, we like the currency and we like their paper, so we are in both. We do not take the same approach in Brazil, because it has too much potential for aggravated inflation. At this point, we are in a defensive posture until we know what happens in the United States—whether we are going to get a continuing series of rate hikes or whether the last rate hike was simply a warning shot from Federal Reserve Board Chair Alan Greenspan.

Question: When you speak of contagion, you are basically saying that analyzing all those exotic currencies in the same way is risky. Is that observation true in practice?

Willner: I refer to contagion as the property that the likelihood of one currency going into crisis (severe devaluation) increases regardless of any relationship between the currencies. Eichengreen et al. (1996) estimated this effect at about 8 percent. Of course, if the currencies are related, say, by location or common markets, that likelihood increases above the contagion percentage. I do not suggest that all exotic currencies be regarded in the same way. Different nations have differences in the factors that determine the stability of those currencies. For instance, trade surplus or deficits, saving rates, currency reserves, and monetary policy are important factors contributing to the stability of currency. I am only suggesting that in addition to evaluating these currencies independently, the investor must be aware of the exogenous risk contagion engenders and ante up the independent country risk measure to account for this risk.

Question: Can we differentiate between one emerging market currency and another? Are some of them better investment choices than others?

Willner: Yes. The answer can be looked at in two dimensions: short term and long term. A short-term outlook would have to be concerned with those factors associated with near-term upgrades or downgrades in the creditworthiness of the country as perceived by rating agencies. Various sovereign-risk models are available from investment banks. These models list factors statistically associated with ability to pay. These factors are not in themselves always sufficient, because they may not reflect government policies and external draws on the currency, but they are a good place to start. Longer term, the direction of the currency depends on the government's ability to stave off inflation and maintain high real yields. Numerous researchers have looked at these issues, and the World Bank sponsors a World Wide Web page with articles on this topic.

Question: With so much electronic currency data, do we get good, complete data?

Willner: My impression from talking to people who actively trade such currencies is that, most of the time, the data presented are reliable, especially with active trading. Not all computer screens regarding a currency are kept current. You must search for the ones that are up to date. During crises, all bets are off (recall the data problems associated with NYSE data during the 1987 crash). Moreover, these markets are not what I would consider truly efficient, and manipulation and corruption have occurred. Develop good contacts and instincts.

Question: What is your guess about the trading techniques to make money—for example, using high-frequency data?

Willner: The emerging market question is not one to be handled by quick trading approaches. First, transacting instantaneously is often difficult in such markets. More importantly, in my opinion, you do not need to do so. Emerging-market currencies are characterized by high returns (look for trending and high real yields) punctuated by bouts of crisis that eat up the high returns and make those markets fair. The best strategy in this scenario is not to try to make a quick buck—the money is accumulating as long as no crisis occurs—but to try to avoid and reduce exposure to crises. For instance, become familiar with the relevant country factors and policies. Reducing exposure is accomplished to a great extent by proper diversification.

To Hedge or Not to Hedge

Mark Lundin
Research Scientist
Olsen & Associates

For investors concerned about risk management, hedging raises important questions involving symmetrical versus asymmetrical hedging and static versus dynamic hedging. Although the effect foreign exchange (FX) risk has on returns depends on the time period, FX-adjusted volatility increases, on average, by 30 percent. Transaction costs provide a threshold effect—the greater the portfolio value at risk, the greater the willingness to pay for complicated hedging strategies. Minimizing value at risk, however, does not always mean full hedging.

The hedging decision is probably one of the most debated topics in international finance, and strong theoretical arguments exist both for and against hedging foreign exchange risk. Opponents of hedging argue that it reduces returns; entails significant transaction costs, rollover risk, and monitoring costs; and increases the correlation of returns. Proponents of hedging argue that hedging reduces portfolio risk and maintains returns of primary investments. No answer is absolutely right or wrong, and perhaps the best approach consists of examining the hedging decision on a case-by-case basis.

This presentation focuses on the decision to hedge and, in general, the trend toward partial hedging.[1] The first section briefly reviews international investment diversification for risk-reduction purposes and the resulting FX risk international diversification introduces. Next, the presentation analyzes static versus dynamic hedging and offers an overview of the goals and constraints of hedging models. Finally, after providing the derivation of foreign investment risk variables and the optimal global static hedge ratio, construction of efficient frontiers for dynamic currency overlay illustrates that minimizing portfolio value at risk does not always mean following a systematic full-hedging policy.

INTERNATIONAL DIVERSIFICATION

Fund managers and financial consumers seek to reduce the risk of their investments through portfolio diversification, but most of these investment opportunities lie outside their domestic markets. **Table 1** lists the major bond markets by size and shows their share of the major-market total. Although Japan and the United States account for a large fraction of fixed-income investment opportunities, no one country has a majority. So, for any home currency, most of the possible fixed-income investments are international in origin.

The situation is much the same for equity markets, as shown in **Table 2**. The United States offers a large share, but not a majority, of equity opportunities, so a large part of possible equity investments are international in origin. These numbers account only generally for the investment opportunities in different countries, but of course, international investors seek assets that do not duplicate those in the domestic market.

Correlations

Potentially beneficial investment opportunities depend on the correlations—or lack thereof—between markets. Low correlations mean that the markets present somewhat independent investment opportunities. According to the data in **Table 3,** world equity markets are correlated, but not highly so. Australia, for example, is only 47 percent correlated with the world equity market and only 44 percent correlated with the U.S. market. Investors seek to reduce volatility or risk in their portfolios through diversification, which implies investing in assets that are not strongly correlated with each other. International investment is one way to achieve

[1] The Olsen & Associates research papers referenced in this presentation are available at the following Internet address: http://www.olsen.ch/library/research/research.html.

Table 1. Locations and Magnitudes of Major Bond Markets

Country	Nominal Value Outstanding (USD billions)	Fraction of Major-Market Total	Date
Japan	$2,630	30.1%	4/96
United States	2,380	27.2	12/31/95
Italy	1,220	13.9	1/31/96
Germany	612	7.0	1/4/96
France	449	5.1	1/31/96
United Kingdom	257	2.9	4/96
Belgium	215	2.5	4/96
Netherlands	200	2.3	4/96
Canada	195	2.2	4/96
Spain	166	1.9	4/96
Denmark	102	1.2	12/31/95
Sweden	85	1.0	4/96
Austria	63	0.7	4/96
Australia	63	0.7	2/29/96
South Africa	42	0.5	1/31/96
Finland	29	0.3	12/31/95
Switzerland	27	0.3	4/96
Ireland	23	0.3	4/96
New Zealand	15	0.2	12/95
Total	8,749	100	

Source: "J.P. Morgan Government Bond Outlines," 9th ed. (April 1996).

Table 2. Locations and Magnitudes of Major Equity Markets

Region and Market	Estimated Equity Market (USD billions)	Fraction of Total
Europe	$3,677	26.2%
United Kingdom	1,328	9.1
Germany	561	3.8
France	489	3.3
Switzerland	390	2.7
Netherlands	292	2.0
Sweden	178	1.2
Italy	165	1.1
Spain	144	1.0
Belgium	97	0.7
Denmark	55	0.4
Finland	46	0.3
Norway	42	0.3
Austria	31	0.2
Ireland	24	0.2
Pacific	4,256	29.0
Japan	3,393	23.1
Hong Kong	262	1.8
Australia	241	1.6
Malaysia	190	1.3
Singapore	138	0.9
New Zealand	32	0.2
North America	6,567	44.8
United States	6,254	42.6
Canada	313	2.1
World	14,665	100.0

Source: "Morgan Stanley Capital International Methodology and Index Policy," November 30, 1995.

Note: Column sums may not total precisely because of rounding.

Table 3. Correlations of Developed Markets' Index Returns in U.S. Dollars with Gross Dividends Reinvested, November 1985–November 1995

	World	Australia	Canada	France	Germany	Hong Kong	Japan	Netherlands	Switzerland	United Kingdom	United States
MSCI World Index	1.00										
Australia	0.47	1.00									
Canada	0.64	0.60	1.00								
France	0.68	0.30	0.39	1.00							
Germany	0.56	0.30	0.33	0.72	1.00						
Hong Kong	0.47	0.50	0.57	0.34	0.35	1.00					
Japan	0.80	0.20	0.29	0.46	0.29	0.15	1.00				
Netherlands	0.77	0.44	0.59	0.67	0.76	0.46	0.45	1.00			
Switzerland	0.70	0.33	0.48	0.60	0.69	0.40	0.41	0.73	1.00		
United Kingdom	0.78	0.51	0.57	0.57	0.51	0.49	0.45	0.75	0.63	1.00	
United States	0.72	0.44	0.72	0.48	0.40	0.46	0.23	0.63	0.55	0.64	1.00

Source: "Morgan Stanley Capital International Methodology and Index Policy," November 30, 1995.

greater diversification. The paradox is that the same diversification that reduces asset risk also introduces another type of risk—foreign exchange risk.

Risk and Return

The effect of foreign exchange (FX) risk on the Standard & Poor's 500 Index and the Dow Jones Industrial Average (DJIA) is shown in **Figure 1,** which compares volatility of the two indexes between 1993 and eary 1996 measured in U.S. dollars and in German marks. The vector time series of the stock index itself multiplied by the FX time series (convolution) increases in volatility during this period, although increased draw-down effects—the maximum loss sustained between any two dates over the lifetime of the investment—are also noticeable.

The returns on these two indexes appear a little lower when measured in foreign currency, a difference that reflects the impact of FX risk. **Table 4** compares returns for these indexes in 10 major currencies. For example, the S&P 500 Index return in Italian lira over this time period was 18.2 percent rather than the 13.5 percent in U.S. dollar terms—a difference of almost 500 basis points. Of course, a different time period might show the exact opposite results because these U.S. stock indexes and FX rates are not highly correlated.

The same cannot be said, however, about volatility. As Table 4 implies, the volatilities of returns increase, on average, more than 30 percent when adjusted for FX risk. The volatilities of returns for the S&P 500 Index and the DJIA measured in U.S. dollars over the 1993 to early 1996 period are 3.7 and 4.2 percent, respectively, but in French francs, for example, the volatilities increased to 5.8 and 6.2 percent. These volatility estimates may appear low because they were calculated using the absolute value of returns (Equation 18 in appendix); the estimates are greater when simple return values are used (Equation 16 in appendix). Nevertheless, the percentage changes in volatilities were measured to be largely independent of the estimation method. The volatility added by exchange rate adjustment is positive for all western European countries and Japan.

With the exception of the Canadian dollar, all FX-adjusted volatilities significantly reduce risk-adjusted returns—on average, by 37 percent measured by the Sharpe ratio. Although Sharpe ratios vary depending on the time period analyzed, these numbers are conservative, because the 1993 to early 1996 period involved high returns for both indexes and, as **Table 5** shows, relatively low FX volatilities. During much of this sample period, the foreign exchange market moved sideways.

CHOOSING TO HEDGE

Managing currency exposure is unavoidable for international investors with more than a small fraction (approximately 5 percent, but it depends on the particular case) of a portfolio dedicated to foreign assets. Investors holding no opinion about currency returns must still make decisions about controlling risk. The hedging decision raises a lot of questions:

- Should the investor hedge symmetrically, minimizing both currency gains and losses with forwards or futures contracts?
- Should the investor hedge asymmetrically, to preserve some currency gains while protecting against currency losses, using option strategies?
- Does the investor want to manage FX risk passively, periodically reexamining a static hedging policy?
- Does the investor want to manage FX risk actively, hedging when returns are unfavorable and decreasing the hedge when returns are favorable?

Currency hedging means that an investor has bought a foreign asset—for example, an equity with a value of S—and holds a short position, $-S_h$, in the foreign currency in order to minimize the volatility of the value of the total investment that results from FX rate fluctuations. The hedging ratio is simply the ratio between values of the short position and the asset:

$$h = \frac{-S_h}{S} \tag{1}$$

A frequently cited study by Froot (1993) shows that choosing the best hedging ratio, the one that minimizes total volatility, is not a trivial decision and depends on the investment horizon. Assuming the hedge ratio is constant over time, the optimal static hedge ratio is probably close to zero for a long investment horizon and probably closer to 1 for a short horizon.

Levich and Thomas (1993a and b) went a step farther than Froot. They hedged a position dynamically by varying hedge ratios over time. This approach intrinsically makes sense because no hedge ratio is always the correct one. A hedge ratio is correct only for any given moment in time. So, the correct, or optimal, hedge ratio is, in fact, a time series. Levich and Thomas showed that an active currency-risk-management strategy—dynamic hedging—is profitable compared with no hedging or static hedging. In one of their most successful strategies, a currency overlay with many currencies involved, they changed the hedge ratios by following simple technical trading signals.

The active, or dynamic, strategy is both the more attractive and the more challenging of the two strat-

Figure 1. S&P 500 Data and DJIA Data Multiplied by the USD/DEM FX Rate

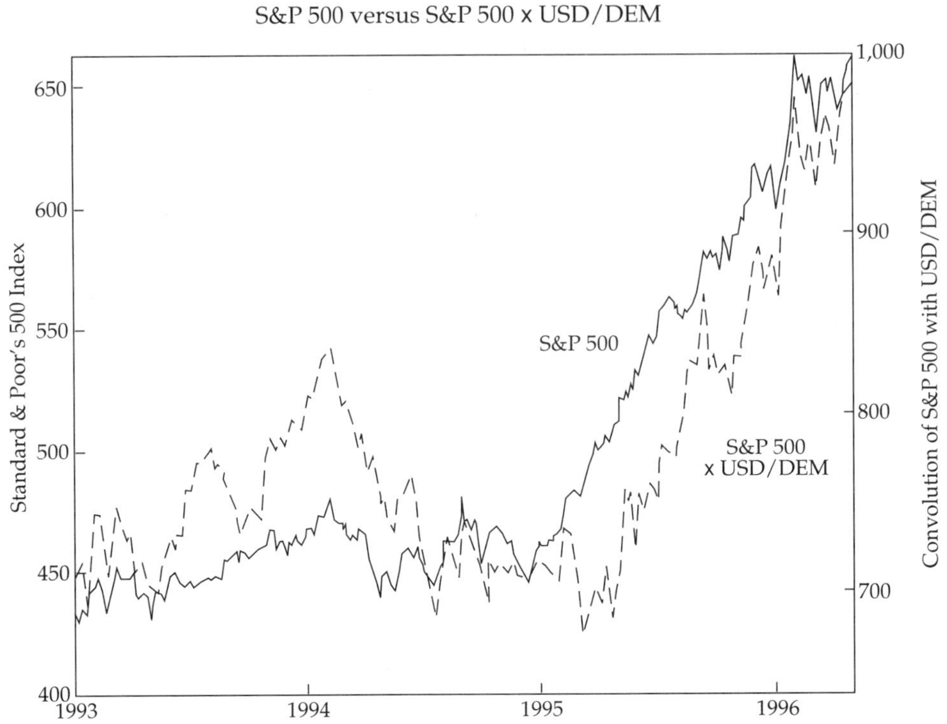

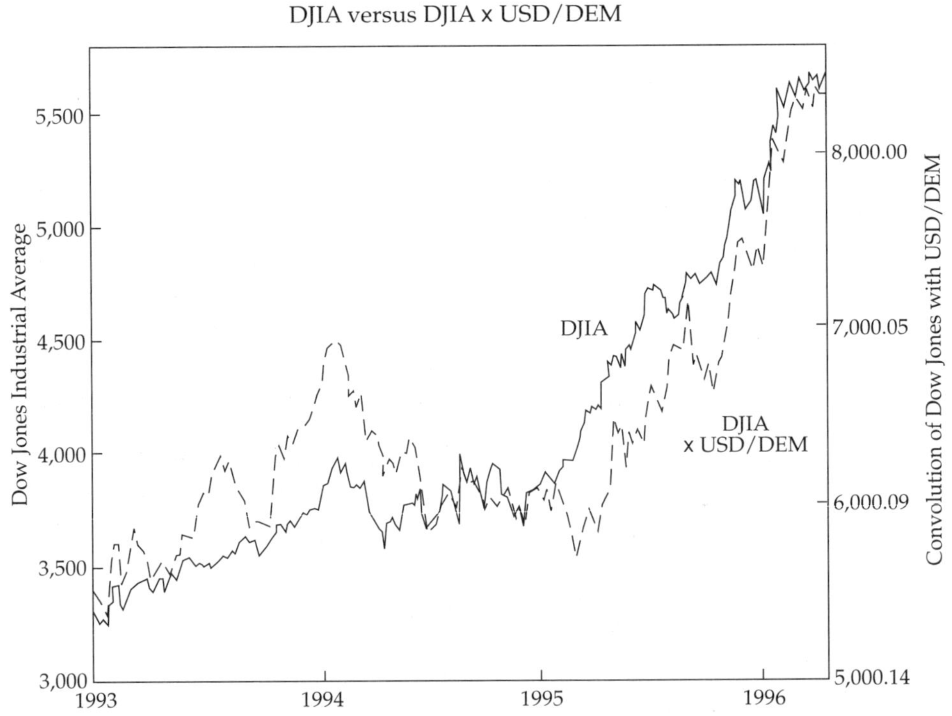

egies. A comparison of the pros and cons of static and dynamic hedging is set forth in **Table 6**. Static hedging provides less adaptability to market changes than does dynamic hedging. Active management tries to increase adaptability, reduce risk, and increase returns, but if the strategy lacks discipline (the ten-

Table 4. FX-Adjusted Returns and Volatilities

Index	Average Annualized Return	Volatility	Added Volatility	Sharpe Ratio	Change in Sharpe Ratio
S&P 500	13.5%	3.7%	0.0%	1.82	0.0%
DJIA	16.9	4.2	0.0	1.75	0.0
S&P 500 ×					
USD/DEM	12.3	6.2	2.5	0.98	–46.0
USD/CHF	9.0	6.6	2.9	0.64	–65.0
USD/FRF	12.3	5.8	2.1	0.95	–48.0
USD/NLG	12.1	6.1	2.4	0.96	–47.0
USD/BEF	12.3	5.7	2.0	0.99	–46.0
USD/JPY	8.2	6.3	2.6	0.59	–68.0
USD/CAD	15.8	4.2	0.5	1.87	2.6
USD/ITL	18.2	5.8	2.1	1.30	–29.0
USD/GBP	14.0	5.5	1.8	1.27	–30.0
USD/ATS	12.3	5.7	2.0	1.08	–41.0
DJIA ×					
USD/DEM	15.7	6.5	2.3	1.12	–36.0
USD/CHF	12.2	6.9	2.7	8.3	–52.0
USD/FRF	15.7	6.2	2.0	1.08	–39.0
USD/NLG	15.5	6.5	2.3	1.10	–37.0
USD/BEF	15.7	6.0	1.8	1.14	–35.0
USD/JPY	11.4	6.6	2.4	0.86	–51.0
USD/CAD	19.3	4.6	0.4	1.78	2.0
USD/ITL	21.7	6.1	1.9	1.39	–20.0
USD/GBP	17.4	5.8	1.6	1.39	–21.0
USD/ATS	15.7	6.2	2.0	1.19	–32.0

dency is to make too many decisions), the investor risks getting whipsawed by the market.

Increased return is almost always a major goal for dynamic hedging, but it is not always a goal for static hedging, because the potential for higher return depends on the situation and the permissible hedging instruments. In dynamic hedging, and to some extent in static hedging, the increased return reflects the gains in FX rates—the reward for doing a bit more work.

Transaction and management costs for static hedging depend on the approach used, but almost any dynamic strategy entails higher transaction costs than static hedging. Of course, the costs depend on the hedging instruments chosen, and that choice depends on what the investor wants to accomplish with the overlay scheme. Transaction costs have a *threshold effect*—the greater the portfolio value at risk, the more investors are willing to pay for complicated strategies. The more complicated the strategy and the better it works, which is not necessarily guaranteed, the more investors will pay for it.

GOALS AND CONSTRAINTS OF TRADING MODELS

Automated trading models are one method for providing discipline, but of course, they must be successful trading models. Many types of trading models are available, each with its own underlying principles and rate of success.

The goal of trading models is to analyze FX movements and generate explicit, real-time trading recommendations that a human trader can execute. System-generated recommendations must be realistic and provide a warning of probable deals a few minutes in advance so that the trader and the model can agree on the price. The model should not change recommendations too rapidly, because that will increase transaction costs. Of course, the model should not give recommendations outside of busi-

Table 5. FX Rate Volatilities: Daily Returns for January 12, 1992, to January 5, 1996

FX Rate	Volatility
USD/DEM	4.3%
USD/CHF	4.8
USD/FRF	3.9
USD/NLG	4.3
USD/BEF	3.9
USD/JPY	4.4
USD/CAD	2.0
USD/ITL	4.0
USD/GBP	3.6
USD/ATS	3.7

Note: Volatility is defined here as the mean of absolute return values taken about the mean.

Table 6. Pros and Cons of Static and Dynamic Hedging

Feature	Static Hedge	Dynamic Hedge
Adaptability to market	Less	More
Reduced risk	Major goal	Major goal
Increased return	Some potential	Major goal
Transaction costs	Depends on strategy	More
Management costs	Depends on strategy	Depends on strategy

ness hours or during market holidays but only when trades can be executed. The model also should support stop-loss around the clock. The ultimate goal is to generate high performance and small capital draw-downs, with performance measured consistently using realistic trading prices.

These goals are clear, but they are difficult to achieve. An example of an Olsen & Associates (O&A) trading model, described in Pictet et al. (1992) and Dacorogna et al. (1995), is shown in **Figure 2**, which illustrates the GBP/DEM time series for January 1996 through December 1996, the actual positions the trading model took, and the total return. These data are from our Model 40. The GBP shows a general upward trend against the DEM during the year (top panel). The trades vary between fully long and fully short, and this particular model works on a discrete gearing system whereby it can take a position of fully long, fully short, neutral, half long, or half short (middle panel). By the end of the year, the model had earned about 12.5 percent (without reinvestment). For the first six months, however, the returns were negative, primarily because of the sideways market early in the year. Still, through a disciplined strategy, the model somehow managed to control its negative returns effectively and to capitalize as much as possible on its positive returns. The average profit for this model was 2.3 percent, and the average loss was 0.8 percent—profit exceeded loss by a factor of three. This ratio is important because technical trading models tend to have more frequent negative return trades than positive ones.

Construction of Trading Models

Because no general theory of market microstructure exists, no definite prescriptions are available for defining indicators or building successful trading models. The market is constantly changing. The strategy to cope with the danger of overfitting is strict discipline in the model-development process, which leads to robust optimization of the model.

An active currency-hedging approach requires systematic discipline. Automated and real-time trading models are one way (but not the only way) to provide this discipline—a dynamic solution that avoids constant management supervision—although some form of constant execution supervision must be maintained.

In a dynamic-hedging approach, the idea is to vary the hedge ratio to what is optimal at any given time. In this way, one attempts to achieve additional returns and reduce the risk of the primary investment expressed in the home currency.

Trading models may also include rules to achieve desirable features; for example, the hedge ratio might be restricted to a desirable range for a given application. The investor can introduce any desired constraints in implementing trading models in a dynamic strategy, but the model must distinguish between the global hedge ratio, h, and the individual hedge ratios, h_i, which are applied to the foreign exchange risk for each of the foreign investments in a portfolio.

Redefined Neutral Point

In the absence of an objective risk criterion, one basic hedging strategy might be the choice of the minimum and maximum allowed global-hedging ratios, h_{min} and h_{max}. For example, choosing a hedge ratio of zero means no hedging and choosing a hedge ratio of -1 means full hedging. The midpoint between the two extreme values represents the neutral point of the portfolio; that is,

$$h = \frac{h_{min} + h_{max}}{2} . \tag{2}$$

The idea is to define a neutral point for the portfolio and trade dynamically around it. The range of dynamic hedging is

$$\Delta h = h_{max} - h_{min} . \tag{3}$$

Portfolio Parameterization

To optimize the hedge ratio and to understand the portfolio's mean–variance characteristics requires a portfolio equation. This equation should include the variables of interest—the underlying assets themselves, the FX rates involved, and the returns and volatilities of any dynamic trading models that are used. An investment portfolio, Π, can be described in terms of the sum of its primary investments, *PI*; the sum of static FX positions or hedges, *SH*; and the sum of variable positions that are placed dynamically to hedge FX risk, *DH*; that is,

$$\Pi = PI + SH + DH . \tag{4}$$

The expectation of portfolio returns, or changes in value, can be written as $E[\Delta\Pi]$ or as the sum of the

Figure 2. O&A Model 40 for GBP/DEM, 1996

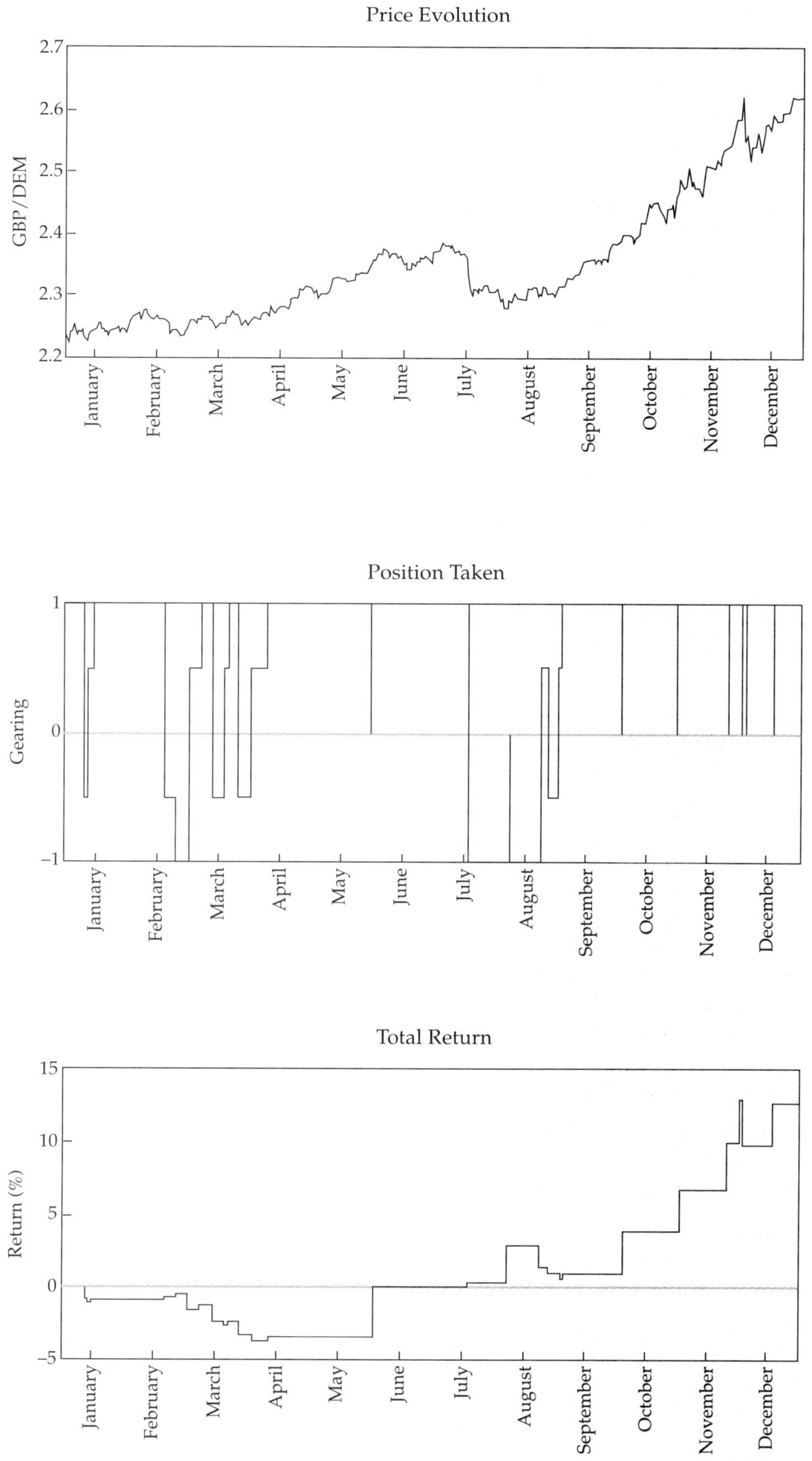

expected values of the individual components:

$$E[\Delta\Pi] = E[\Delta I] + E[\Delta R^{FX}] + E[\Delta R^{TM}] . \quad (5)$$

In the following expressions, the underlying investments are the sum of the weights given to each primary investment; the sum of FX positions, where h refers to the level to which these FX positions are hedged; and the sum of the weights given to each trading model (all variables are in units of the home currency):

$$\Delta I = \sum_{i=1}^{n} \alpha_i \Delta I_i \, ; \, E[\Delta I] = \sum_{i=1}^{n} \alpha_i E[\Delta I_i] ,$$

$$\Delta R^{FX} = \sum_{i=1}^{n} h_i \alpha_i \Delta R_i^{FX}; \, E[R^{FX}] = \sum_{i=1}^{n} h_i \alpha_i E[\Delta R_i^{FX}] ,$$

$$\Delta R^{TM} = \sum_{j=1}^{m} \omega_j \Delta R_j^{TM}; \, E[R^{TM}] = \sum_{j=1}^{m} \omega_j E[\Delta R_j^{TM}] , \quad (6)$$

where

ΔI_i = the fractional return of the ith underlying foreign investment component at a given time, t, and over a time horizon, $\Delta I_i \equiv \Delta I_i \Delta t, t) \equiv (I_t - I_{t-\Delta_t}) / I_{t-\Delta_t}$

α_i = the amount of the portfolio allocated to the ith currency

h_i = the unitless static hedging ratio for the ith foreign currency

ΔR_i^{FX} = the portfolio returns resulting from fluctuations in the static hedge positions

ω_j = the weights given to each trading model

ΔR_j^{TM} = the trading model return values

The expected return of the portfolio is the sum of the expected returns of the individual components:

$$E[\Delta\Pi] = \sum_{i=1}^{n} \alpha_i E[\Delta I_i] + \sum_{i=1}^{n} h_i \alpha_i E[\Delta R_i^{FX}] + \sum_{j=1}^{m} \omega_j E[\Delta R_j^{TM}] \quad (7)$$

More importantly, the variance, or risk, of portfolio returns, $\sigma^2_{\Delta\Pi}$, can be written as the difference between individual return values and expected return values of the underlying investments, *PI;* statically hedged, *SH,* components; and dynamically hedged, *DH,* components:

$$\begin{aligned}\sigma^2_{\Delta\Pi} &= E[(\Delta\Pi - E[\Delta\Pi])^2] \\ &= E\left[\left((\Delta I - E[\Delta I]) + (\Delta R^{FX} - E[\Delta R^{FX}]) + (\Delta R^{TM} - E[\Delta R^{TM}])\right)^2\right] . \quad (8)\end{aligned}$$

The following definitions are introduced for simplification:

$$\begin{aligned}\Delta I' &= \Delta I - E[\Delta I] , \\ \Delta R'_{FX} &= \Delta R_{FX} - E[\Delta R_{FX}] , \\ \Delta R'_{TM} &= \Delta R_{TM} - E[\Delta R_{TM}] . \quad (9)\end{aligned}$$

As a result of these simplifications, the variance of the portfolio returns can be written in terms of the variances of the individual components—the underlying investment, the static hedge, and the dynamic hedge—and how the different portfolio components work together and contribute to overall volatility. Thus, the correlation between the components provides the framework for optimized dynamic currency overlays using trading models:

$$\begin{aligned}\sigma^2_{\Delta\Pi} &= E[(\Delta I' + \Delta R'_{FX} + \Delta R'_{TM})^2] \\ &= E[(\Delta I')^2] + E[(\Delta R'_{FX})^2] + E[(\Delta R'_{TM})^2] \\ &+ 2\rho(I, FX)\sqrt{E[(\Delta I')^2]E[(\Delta R'_{FX})^2]} \\ &+ 2\rho(I, TM)\sqrt{E[(\Delta I')^2]E[(\Delta R'_{TM})^2]} \\ &+ 2\rho(FX, TM)\sqrt{E[(\Delta R'_{FX})^2]E[(\Delta R'_{TM})^2]} \quad (10)\end{aligned}$$

where correlations between the underlying investments and FX, between underlying investments and trading models, and between FX and trading models are defined as follows:

$$\rho(I, FX) = \frac{E[\Delta I' \Delta R'_{FX}]}{\sqrt{E[(\Delta I')^2]E[(\Delta R'_{FX})^2]}} ,$$

$$\rho(I, TM) = \frac{E[\Delta I' \Delta R'_{TM}]}{\sqrt{E[(\Delta I')^2]E[(\Delta R'_{TM})^2]}} ,$$

$$\rho(FX, TM) = \frac{E[\Delta R'_{FX} \Delta R'_{TM}]}{\sqrt{E[(\Delta R'_{FX})^2]E[(\Delta R'_{TM})^2]}} .$$

Equation 10 uses trading models to give the framework for optimizing dynamic currency overlays. To avoid trading models, set to zero the terms that involve trading models.

Investors can find the optimal static hedging ratio by assuming that the trading models are not used. The portfolio variance in the absence of trading model variance is reduced to the variances of the underlying investment and the static hedge and the correlation between them, as follows:

$$\sigma^2_{\Delta\Pi;\,stat} = E[(\Delta I')^2] + E[(\Delta R'_{FX})^2] + 2\rho(I, FX)\sqrt{E[(\Delta I')^2]E[(\Delta R'_{FX})^2]} \quad (11)$$

A Global Static Hedging Ratio

To arrive at a closed expression for the global static hedging ratio, assume that all the currency-related hedge ratios, h_i, are equal to the global hedge ratio, h, as yet unknown. Each h_i is equal to the hedging ratio for each currency and is exactly the same as for another currency, and they are all then equal to a global hedging ratio. That assumption is used to arrive at a closed solution, but this solution can be expanded without losing any generalities.

It is then easy to verify that

$$E[(\Delta R'_{FX})^2] = h^2\sigma^2_{FX}, \quad (12)$$

where

$$\sigma^2_{FX} \equiv E\left[\left(\sum_{i=1}^{n}\alpha_i(\Delta R_{FX,\,i} - E[\Delta R_{FX,\,i}])\right)^2\right].$$

Similarly, if we define $E[(\Delta I')^2] \equiv \sigma^2_I$, we can write the portfolio variance in terms of a simple algebraic formula:

$$\begin{aligned}\sigma^2_{\Delta\Pi} &= \sigma^2_I + h^2\sigma^2_{FX} + 2\rho(I, FX)(\sigma^2_I h^2\sigma^2_{FX})^{1/2}\\ &= \sigma^2_I + h^2\sigma^2_{FX} + 2h\sigma_I\sigma_{FX}\rho(I, FX)\,. \quad (13)\end{aligned}$$

The most commonly accepted purpose of hedging is to reduce the risk of the primary investment expressed in the home currency. Thus, the optimal static hedge ratio can be found by minimizing the variance of the portfolio with respect to h:

$$\frac{d\sigma^2_{\Delta\Pi}}{dh} = 2h\sigma^2_{FX} + 2\rho(I, FX)\sigma_I\sigma_{FX},$$

$$\left(\frac{d\sigma^2_{\Delta\Pi}}{dh}\right)_{\min} = 0 = h\sigma_{FX} + \rho(I, FX)\sigma_I\,. \quad (14)$$

The result is an elegant equation that expresses the optimized global static hedge ratio:

$$h = -\rho(I, FX)\frac{\sigma_I}{\sigma_{FX}}\,. \quad (15)$$

This equation is simply the correlation between the underlying investments and FX fluctuations multiplied by the ratio of standard deviations of the underlying investments and the FX itself. Even in the derivation, we arrive at a negative sign, indicating short positions to be taken.

Several observations can be drawn from this equation. First, if we want to optimize the portfolio value at risk, a hedging ratio of –1.0 is not necessarily optimal. Second, if the correlation between the underlying investments and FX equals zero, then FX may provide further portfolio diversification and no hedge is recommended. For the sake of completeness, keep in mind that we assume that the best static hedging ratio for a foreign portfolio component is equal to the most straightforward definition—for every i, $h_i = h$.

In almost all cases, one can make at least a second-order improvement on this result by reworking the derivation without this assumption, thus arriving at a solution involving individual static hedging ratios for each different currency in the set of primary investments. Depending on the quality of the data used in the calculation (historical versus good forecast), this improvement may be lost in the systematic error of optimal hedging estimation. Perhaps as important, though, in many cases the calculation of individual static hedging ratios can reduce transaction costs with the same or slightly better expected portfolio performance, because individual cross-rate pairs with less volatility will be allowed to go unhedged.

EFFICIENT FRONTIER GENERATION

Once we have the equation for expected return of a portfolio and the equation for its expected variance, we have the equivalent choice between maximizing risk-adjusted portfolio returns, $E[\Delta\Pi] - \lambda\sigma^2_{\Delta\Pi^3}$, or minimizing return-adjusted risk, $\lambda\sigma^2_{\Delta\Pi} - E[\Delta\Pi]$, where λ is a constrained minimization multiplier, which can be varied to get any combination of desired portfolio characteristics on the entire efficient frontier. The exact way in which this procedure is done depends on the financial instruments involved. One might consider the stability over time of the distribution's mean and variance and whether or not historical data or data from a good forecast are used. Relying heavily on increased returns is not very helpful if the expected value of mean returns has a large error.

Efficient Frontiers for Dynamic Overlays

Given the neutral point of the statically hedged portfolio, expected portfolio returns, variances, correlations, and the exact choice of mean–variance optimization methodology, any number of mathematical tools can be used to generate a large set of possible investment portfolios. The set of feasible portfolios available to an investor implementing a currency-hedging strategy is depicted in **Figure 3**. If we know the optimal static hedge ratio, we probably can reduce the risk of the original unhedged primary

Figure 3. Efficient Frontier Generation

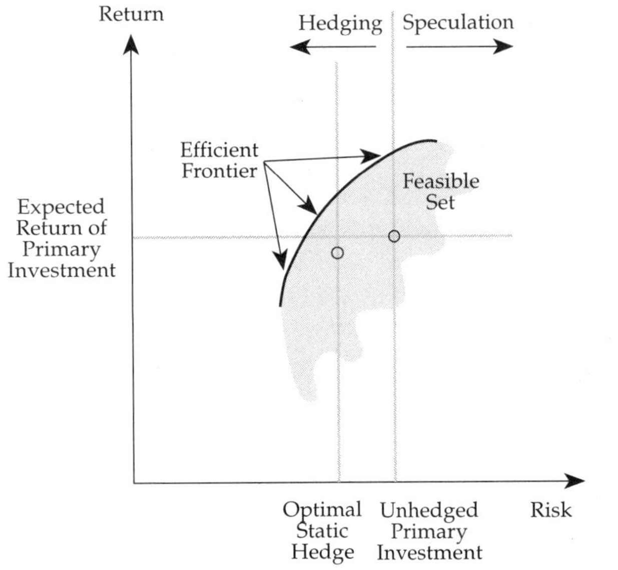

Figure 4. Efficient Frontier for Dynamic Overlay: Guilder-Based Investor

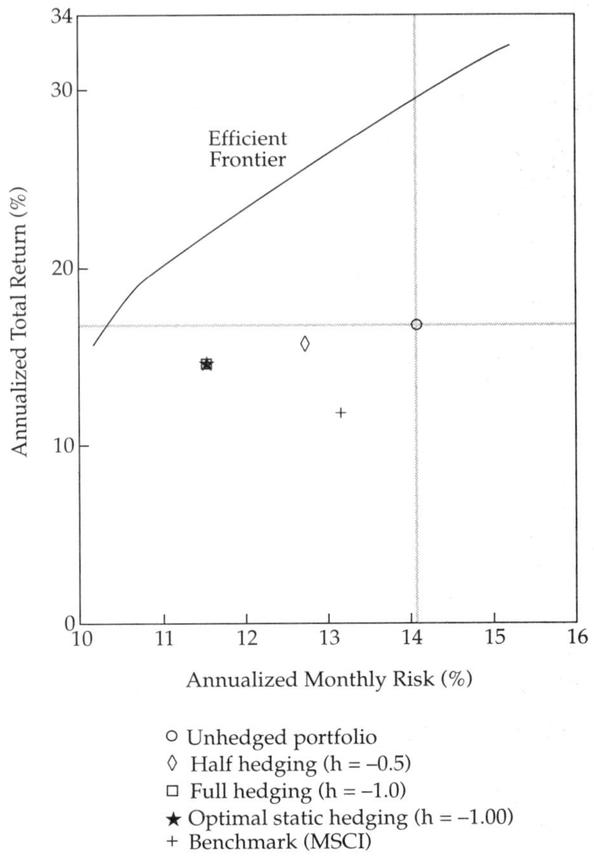

investment position—perhaps at the cost of a small reduction in return to account for transaction and management costs. By using trading models in an active currency overlay scheme, however, we at least hope to find a vector that moves toward the actual efficient frontier. Each point on this efficient frontier corresponds to a different portfolio of trading models or a different dynamic overlay strategy. The choice of a portfolio on the efficient frontier is based on the investor's risk–return preferences.

For example, the portfolio of a Netherlands guilder-based investor holding an internationally diversified portfolio of equity indexes is shown in **Table 7**. Using historical data, optimization of Equations 7 and 10 yields the expected mean–variance-efficient frontier, shown in **Figure 4**, in which all returns are above the home currency risk-free interest rate. By assuming an additional 1 percent extra in risk, the investor receives about 5 percent additional return relative to the benchmark MSCI World Index by choosing the unhedged portfolio, but in this case, the optimal global static hedge ratio is –1.0, a full hedge. Between optimal static hedging and no hedging is the static half-hedging position. In this example, any static hedging of the initial primary (unhedged) portfolio succeeds in reducing risk, but the investor pays a small price in terms of reduced return.

Table 7. Guilder-Based Investor

Foreign Currency	Amount (NLG millions)	Investment
DEM	175	Deutscher Aktienindex (DAX)
USD	125	DJIA
FRF	75	Cotation Assistée en Continu (CAC 40)
ITL	50	Banca Commerciale Italiana General (BCIG)
CHF	25	Swiss Market Index (SMI)
JPY	25	Nikkei 225
SEK	25	Stockholm General Index (SGI)

A similar analysis for a British pound-based investor involved in various international stock indexes is shown in **Table 8** and **Figure 5**. The fully hedged portfolio yields significantly greater returns than both the unhedged portfolio and the benchmark MSCI Index, but at the cost of significantlygreater risk. This investor's optimal static hedge ratio is –0.31, which demonstrates that minimizing the portfolio's

Table 8 Pound-Based Investor

Foreign Currency	Amount (GBP millions)	Investment
USD	20	S&P 500
DEM	20	DAX
CHF	10	SMI
FRF	10	CAC 40
ITL	10	BCIG
SEK	10	SGI
NLG	10	Amsterdam EOE Index (AEX)
BEF	5	Belgium 20 Index (Bel 20)
JPY	5	Nikkei 225

Figure 5. Efficient Frontier for Dynamic Overlay: Pound-Based Investor

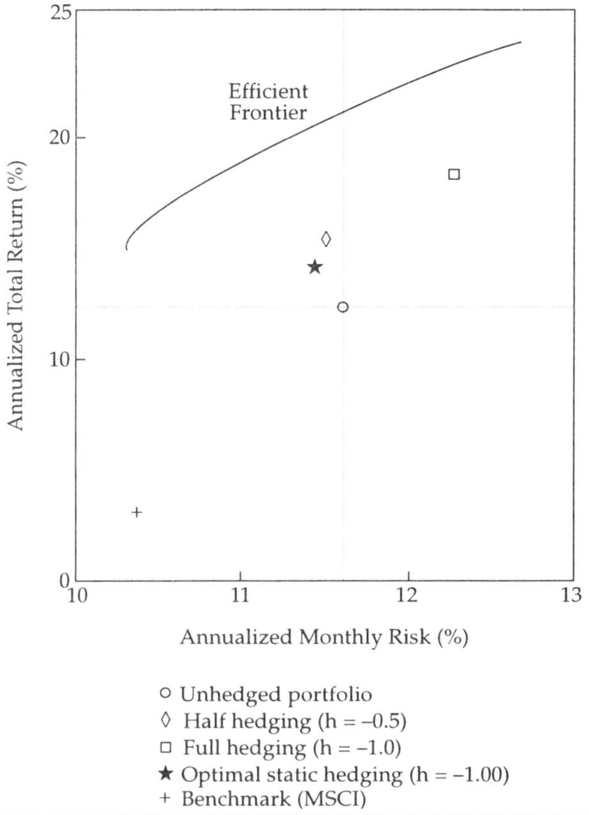

value at risk does not always entail full hedging.

These examples use the actual return and variance characteristics from real-time FX trading models and illustrate how investors might combine any such dynamic portfolio elements with the underlying, essentially static, portfolio elements in an attempt to optimize performance.

To establish the optimized variance or risk of an overlay product, we must know the correlations between the underlying portfolio itself and FX returns, between FX returns and trading model returns, and between underlying portfolio returns and trading model returns. The correlations between these items are the most critical terms in the optimized global hedging equation. Much of this correlation information already exists in financial literature. The linear correlation coefficient is not completely suitable for time series distributed in a non-Gaussian fashion, but it remains to a large extent a descriptive and meaningful measure of correlations between financial time series. This limitation is especially the case for lower frequency (i.e., daily data) financial time series whose leptokurticity is very often proportional to data frequency.

CONCLUSION

Investors seek to reduce the volatility of their portfolios through diversification. International investment is a necessary prerequisite for greater diversification, but the paradox is that volatility-reducing diversification introduces another type of risk emanating from FX fluctuations. Such fluctuations increase portfolio volatility, on average, by more than 30 percent, reducing risk-adjusted returns by a factor of two as measured by FX-adjusted Sharpe ratios.

The volatility added by currency fluctuations is too much to ignore, and the resulting risk must be hedged in some way. How to hedge this risk depends on an investor's risk tolerance, and it is best done on a case-by-case basis.

Passive-management studies tell us that the optimal hedging ratio depends on the investor's time horizon and on FX and primary investment correlations and volatility ratios. A study by Froot indicates that short-term investors should remain closer to fully hedged whereas investors with very long time frames should lean more toward unhedged postions. One example of a dynamic portfolio design was used to illustrate how active portfolio managers might choose an overlay hedging strategy according to their particular underlying portfolios and their risk–return appetites.

APPENDIX: DEFINITION OF VOLATILITY AND SHARPE (RETURN–RISK) RATIO

Data sets of daily stock indexes and FX returns were obtained to use in volatility calculations. These returns, defined as in Guillaume et al. (1994), are

$$r(t_i) \equiv r(\Delta t; t_i) \equiv [x(t_i) - x(t_i - \Delta)], \qquad (16)$$

where Δt is a fixed time interval (or time solution) and $x(t_i)$ is the sequence of logarithmic prices, equally spaced in time. $x(t_i)$ is calculated as follows from the average of the logarithmic bid and ask prices (p_{bid} and p_{ask}, respectively):

$$x(t_i) \equiv x(\Delta t; t_i) \equiv [\log p_{ask}(t_i) + \log p_{bid}(t_i)]/2. \qquad (17)$$

Stock index, currency foreign exchange, and convolution (indexes × FX) return values were analyzed for volatility. The volatility at t_i, $v(t_i)$ is defined as

$$v(t_i) \equiv v(\Delta t, S; t_i) \equiv \frac{1}{n} \sum_{k=1}^{n} \left| r(\Delta t; t_{i-k}) \right|, \qquad (18)$$

where S is the sample period on which the volatility was computed (1/12/92 to 1/5/96), and n is a positive integer with $S = n\Delta t$ (here, Δt = 1 day). As with stock index values themselves, return values for stock indexes measured in non-USD currencies are obtained through the product of an index return value with an FX return value. Volatility values reported here are the annualized ($\times\sqrt{250}$) average daily volatilities over the entire time period, S.

In addition to volatility, time series were analyzed for their annualized return–risk quotients, often referred to as Sharpe ratios. For this discussion, we define the Sharpe ratio on a monthly basis as follows:

$$R_s \equiv \frac{\bar{R}_m}{\sigma_{R_m}} \times \sqrt{12} \equiv \frac{\frac{1}{N}\sum_{i=1}^{N} R_i}{\sqrt{\frac{\sum_{i=1}^{N}(R_i - \bar{R}_m)^2}{N}}} \times \sqrt{12}, \tag{19}$$

where $\bar{R}_m$ is mean value of N monthly (nonlog) returns (R_i) and σ_{R_m} is the square root of the variance of those same returns. Taking a stock index as an example, our definition dictates that we first obtain the 42 monthly returns during the period from January 1, 1992, to January 5, 1996. These values are nothing more than the difference between the index values at the end and beginning of a given month. The Sharpe ratio is then equal to the mean value of the 42 returns divided by the square root of the variance of the same set. All ratios reported here are as defined after having been annualized ($\times\sqrt{12}$).

Question and Answer Session

Mark C. Lundin

Question: When you say one should systematically hedge FX, should you also differentiate between the bond and equity portfolio components?

Lundin: I drew the conclusion that hedging is necessary, but I cannot give a quantitative answer at this moment as to how I feel about equities versus fixed-income instruments. I would put the volatilities and correlations of the different instruments into the expectation-values equation and let them work themselves out. I would certainly treat them differently, but treat them differently as prescribed by these equations.

Question: How do you deal with the issue of multinational companies, which certainly make their own hedging calls, within the context of a global equity portfolio?

Lundin: This problem requires a case-by-case solution. What is the corporation's home currency? Does such a thing as a home currency truly exist? These considerations make the problem even more complicated, and it is not a unique problem.

Question: Do you have a view on the minimum-size portfolio for which to apply dynamic techniques?

Lundin: The minimum size depends on your objectives and constraints. Portfolio managers subject to institutional constraints hedge simply to lessen portfolio value at risk so that they can reduce the amount of capital reserves they are forced to hold—even if they are dealing with negligible amounts of money compared with other areas they actively manage. A linear relationship probably exists between the amount under management and the willingness to spend money on more complicated hedging strategies.

A portfolio-dependent threshold probably often exists. Below this threshold—usually 5 percent—foreign exchange volatility acts as a new asset class, which reduces volatility via a diversification effect.

Question: How stable is the optimal hedge ratio over time, and how much does its stability depend on the investor's base currency?

Lundin: Optimal hedging ratios tend to be more stable over time than return values because they are based on more stable variances and covariances. The degree of stability varies on a case-by-case basis. Also, the variances of the underlying portfolio play a part, but the FX rates themselves are primarily responsible. Over time, at least for industrialized countries, the correlations between FX rates tend to be quite stable. For instance, USD/DEM, USD/FRF, and USD/NLG tend to be highly stable, with linear correlation coefficients exceeding 90 percent.

Exceptions to high correlations exist, however. For instance, the Italian lira measured in U.S. dollars is highly correlated to USD/DEM, but in fact, the correlation relationship breaks down at times. For instance, in the latter part of 1992, when the lira and the pound took a step back from monetary union, correlations distinctly dropped.

Question: If we can develop all those models and implement those techniques, why have a human trader?

Lundin: Some people want the human interface. Consensus says that people want, at least for security reasons, the possibility for human intervention. The reason may be that the people on the FX desks may be qualified, have relationships with market makers, and know who to call to obtain the best price. The interface between computer automated trading system and actual execution sequence is probably quite complex and needs the human touch.

Strategies for Hedging

Mark P. Kritzman, CFA
Partner
Windham Capital Management

Simultaneously maximizing absolute returns on an underlying portfolio and relative returns on a currency benchmark moves global investors from the efficient frontier to the efficient surface. This joint optimization in three dimensions—expected return, volatility, and tracking error—almost always produces better results than constrained mean–variance analysis. Nonlinear hedging strategies are an effective method for managing currency risk, but obtaining some of these instruments—contingent currency options and hybrid collars—can be difficult and expensive.

Determining the appropriate hedging strategy involves understanding the motivation for currency-risk management, knowing that the relevant correlation is that between foreign asset returns in the investor's base currency and currency returns, evaluating linear and nonlinear hedging strategies and available hedging instruments (forwards, traditional options, contingent options, and hybrid collars), and assessing the cash flow implications of currency-hedging strategies.

Although the motivation for currency-risk management is to maximize expected utility, institutional investors may seek to define utility in absolute terms, relative terms, or both. How a currency's correlation with local foreign asset returns is mapped onto its correlation with base-currency-denominated foreign asset returns significantly affects the minimum-risk hedge ratio. Determining the appropriate hedging strategy requires not only understanding available instruments but also evaluating strategies—especially nonlinear strategies—against a relevant benchmark. Analyzing currency-hedging strategies using value-at-risk analysis can help estimate cash flow demands at various confidence levels for a currency overlay portfolio.

MOTIVATION FOR CURRENCY-RISK MANAGEMENT

The objective of currency-risk management is to maximize expected utility, which traditionally has been defined as expected return minus risk aversion times variance, or

$$R_P + R_f \times W - A(S_p^2 + S_f^2 \times W^2 + 2 \times r \times S_p \times S_f \times W),$$

where

R_p = the portfolio's return
R_f = return of a currency forward contract
W = weighting in the forward contract
A = index of risk aversion
S_p = standard deviation of the portfolio
S_f = standard deviation of currency
r = correlation between portfolio returns and currency returns

For an investor who is infinitely risk averse (has a high risk-aversion index factor), the optimal hedge ratio is minus the correlation between portfolio returns and currency returns multiplied by the ratio of the portfolio standard deviation and the currency standard deviation, or $W = -r(S_p/S_f)$. To solve for the optimal hedge ratio, an investor who believes in uncovered interest arbitrage—that is, one who believes that the forward rate is an unbiased predictor of the future spot rate—would simply set the return of the forward contract equal to the hedging cost. This approach presumes that the investor is selling forward contracts only to hedge existing currency exposure. Alternatively, an investor who believes that the current spot rate is the unbiased predictor of the future spot rate would condition the expected return on the forward contract by the discount (positive return) or the premium (negative return). Such an investor would hedge less when the currency sells at a discount and hedge more when it sells at a premium.

CURRENCY EXPOSURE AND DIVERSIFICATION

Many U.S. investors believe that they are diversified

by investing overseas and that currencies give them exposure that should not be hedged away. I disagree with that view. Although currency returns may have a low or negative correlation with local foreign-asset returns, the relevant correlation is between currency returns and the foreign-asset returns denominated in the base currency. A U.S. investor should not care about the correlation between, say, the yen and the local return of Japanese stocks but should care about the correlation between the dollar-denominated return of Japanese stocks and yen currency returns. Many investors, believing that hedging introduces diversification, instead look at the correlation between the yen and the local return of Japanese stocks and note that it is either zero or negative.

The following equation shows how a currency's correlation with local foreign-asset returns is mapped onto its correlation with base-currency-denominated foreign-asset returns:

$$R_B = \frac{R_L + S_L + S_C}{(S_L^2 + S_C^2 + 2 \times R_L \times S_L \times S_C)^{1/2}},$$

where

R_B = base-currency foreign-asset returns

R_L = local returns

S_L = standard deviation of local asset returns

S_C = standard deviation of currency returns

S_L^2 = variance of local asset returns

S_C^2 = variance of currency returns

Table 1 provides examples of how the minimum-risk hedge ratio fluctuates. The ratios shown assume that both the currency and the portfolio have standard deviations equal to 10 percent, which is reasonable for many major currencies. A 50 percent correlation between local returns and the currency translates into an 87 percent correlation between U.S. dollar-denominated returns and the currency, resulting in a minimum-risk hedge ratio of 150 percent. If the correlation between local returns and the currency is 0 percent, the correlation between dollar-denominated returns and the currency is still 71 percent. If the correlation between local returns and the currency is –50 percent, the correlation between dollar-denominated returns and the currency is still 50 percent.

Table 1. Currency Correlations and Minimum Hedge Ratios

Currency Correlations		
Local	Base	Minimum-Risk Hedge Ratio[a]
50%	87%	150%
0	71	100
–50	50	50
–100	0	0

[a]Assumes local return standard deviation and currency standard deviation both equal 10 percent.

So, taking the correlation into account, currency exposure does not provide a lot of diversification. Correlation significantly affects the minimum-risk hedge ratio. Few foreign portfolios have enough diversification between the currency and the base-currency-denominated assets of that portfolio to make the argument that diversification is overcoming the volatility that currency exposure introduces in the portfolio. The only situation in which an investor would not hedge currency exposure to minimize risk is the case in which the currency is believed to have a significantly negative correlation with the domestic assets in the portfolio and a large fraction of that portfolio is allocated to domestic assets. In that case, the correlation may be weak enough to overcome the high positive correlation that currencies will always have with the foreign assets in the portfolio.

LINEAR CURRENCY-HEDGING STRATEGIES

Investors have traditionally used mean–variance optimization, which attempts to maximize their utility by providing the highest return for a given level of risk or the lowest risk for a given return. Alternatively, many investors are faced with maximizing other utility functions—for example, outperforming their benchmark, expressed as maximizing the result of the following equation:

$$\text{Expected return} - \text{Tracking-error aversion} \times \text{Tracking error}^2.$$

An Endowment Application

One innovation is a situation in which both absolute volatility and relative volatility are examined simultaneously in the optimization process. For example, if an institution wants to outperform both an absolute and a relative benchmark, it needs to maximize the following:

$$\text{Expected return} - \text{Risk aversion} \times \text{Variance} - \text{Tracking-error aversion} \times \text{Tracking error}^2.$$

This idea was motivated by a major university's asset allocation analysis for its endowment fund. The fund was faced with two targets—an absolute target and a relative target. It was expected to achieve a rate of return sufficient to meet the university's spending plan—the absolute target—and at the same time, it was expected to outperform the endowments of competing universities. It had a formal investment objective of outperforming a composite portfolio that consisted of several universities, but not just as an issue of pride or some notion of keeping score. Even if its funds were to do well in an absolute sense by consistently achieving a rate of return greater than the spending plan, if it underperformed relative to schools with which it competed for faculty, students, and funding, then it would be at a competitive disadvantage. So, one could argue that underperformance has an economic consequence.

Efficient Frontier versus Efficient Surface

The traditional efficient frontier has only two dimensions, but if absolute and relative returns are both important, we get an efficient surface in three dimensions—expected return, standard deviation, and tracking error—as shown in **Figure 1**. The bottom left corner of the surface represents the minimum-risk portfolio, the U.S. Treasury bill portfolio. The benchmark portfolio, which has zero tracking error, is represented by a line from the top right corner of the surface down to the tracking-error dimension, which is represented by the benchmark portfolio. The lower boundary of this efficient surface, therefore, consists of linear combinations of the minimum-risk portfolio and the benchmark portfolio. The upper left boundary is the traditional mean–variance-efficient frontier, and the boundary to the right is the mean-tracking-error-efficient frontier. All of the portfolios on the surface are efficient in all three dimensions.

The ideal outcome for the university endowment fund is that it outperform both the absolute target and the benchmark. Another outcome is that the fund outperform the absolute target but underperform the benchmark, or the converse: to outperform the benchmark but underperform the absolute target. The most unpleasant outcome—particularly worrisome to the university—is the situation in which the endowment underperforms both the absolute target and the benchmark. The endowment would be in big trouble if it fell short of the spending plan *and* fell behind competing schools at the same time.

Adding a currency benchmark to a portfolio benchmark provides an absolute target on an underlying portfolio and a currency target. After expending a lot of energy and anguish to persuade the investment committee to invest overseas, a fund sponsor would be embarrassed if those investments were to perform poorly in their local markets and also experience currency losses.

Figure 1. The Efficient Currency-Hedging Surface

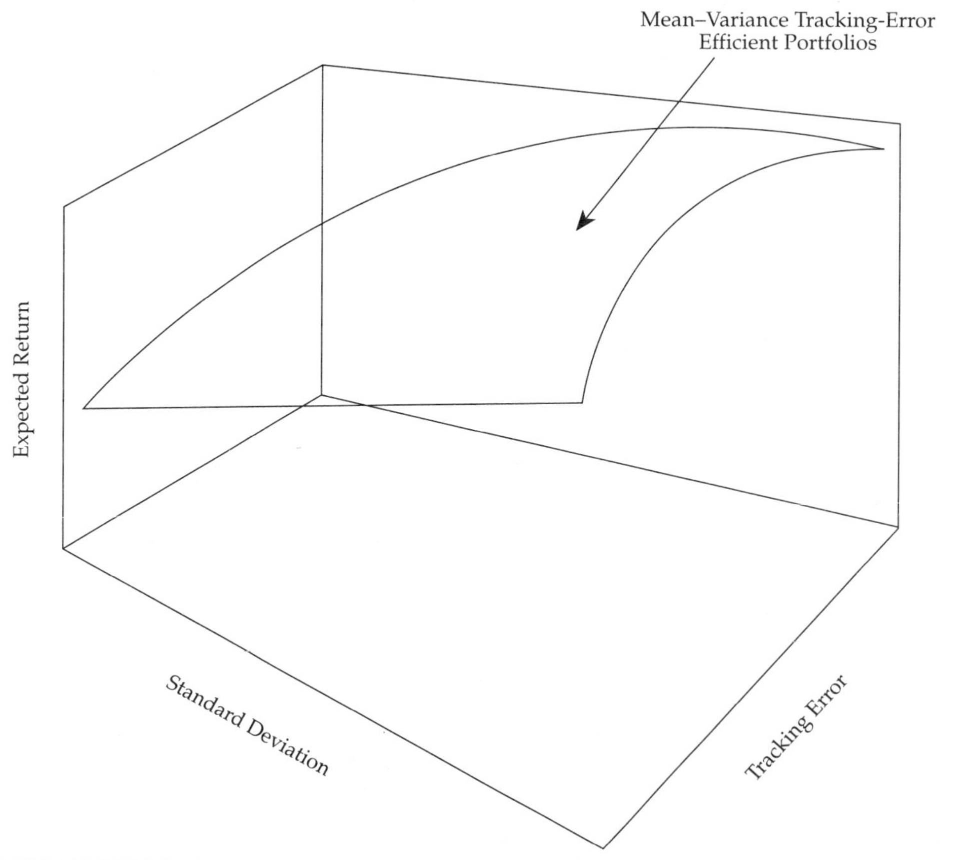

Mean–Variance Tracking-Error Optimization

Rather than dealing with the traditional bell-shaped curve (i.e., the normal distribution or lognormal distribution), we are dealing with joint probability estimation, because risk has two dimensions—absolute risk and relative risk or currency risk—as shown in **Figure 2**. Concern about the probability of underperforming the absolute target requires slicing the bell at the absolute return axis, as shown in **Figure 3**. The area to the left represents the probability of underperforming the absolute target return—in this case, 6.5 percent. Concern about relative return requires slicing the bell on that axis, and in this case, the target currency return is 0 percent. The raised area in **Figure 4** represents the probability of underperforming the benchmark. **Figure 5** illustrates the probability of underperforming the currency benchmark and simultaneously experiencing an absolute target shortfall.

This approach, called mean–variance tracking-error (MVTE) optimization, deals simultaneously with both an absolute benchmark and a currency benchmark, almost always producing better results than a traditional constrained mean–variance analysis. Mean–variance constraints may include not hedging, hedging specific currencies, not hedging more than 100 percent or less than 0 percent of a currency, or limitations on foreign investments. MVTE optimization almost always produces a higher expected return with the same level of standard deviation and tracking error, a lower standard deviation of returns at the same level of expected return and tracking error, or less tracking error at the same level of expected return and standard deviation. This outcome has to be true unless the optimal constraints are known ahead of time, which of course, they are not.

When using the optimizer, think of risk aversion and tracking-error aversion as dials that can be turned up or down to show different regions of the efficient surface. The way to choose a particular hedging policy is by calculating the probability of achieving or failing to achieve outcomes that are important to the investor. For example, if an important objective is not falling behind the benchmark and losing money at the same time, compare different hedging strategies based on the joint probability of that occurrence. So, tracking-error tolerance need not be specified explicitly. Simply look at portfolios that have different combinations of risk tolerance and tracking-error tolerance and evaluate the probabilities that those portfolios will achieve the desired targets. How much tracking-error efficiency one gives up depends on the specific portfolio.

This approach enables one to produce an "iso-expected-return curve"—that is, a curve that shows

Figure 2. Joint Probability Estimation

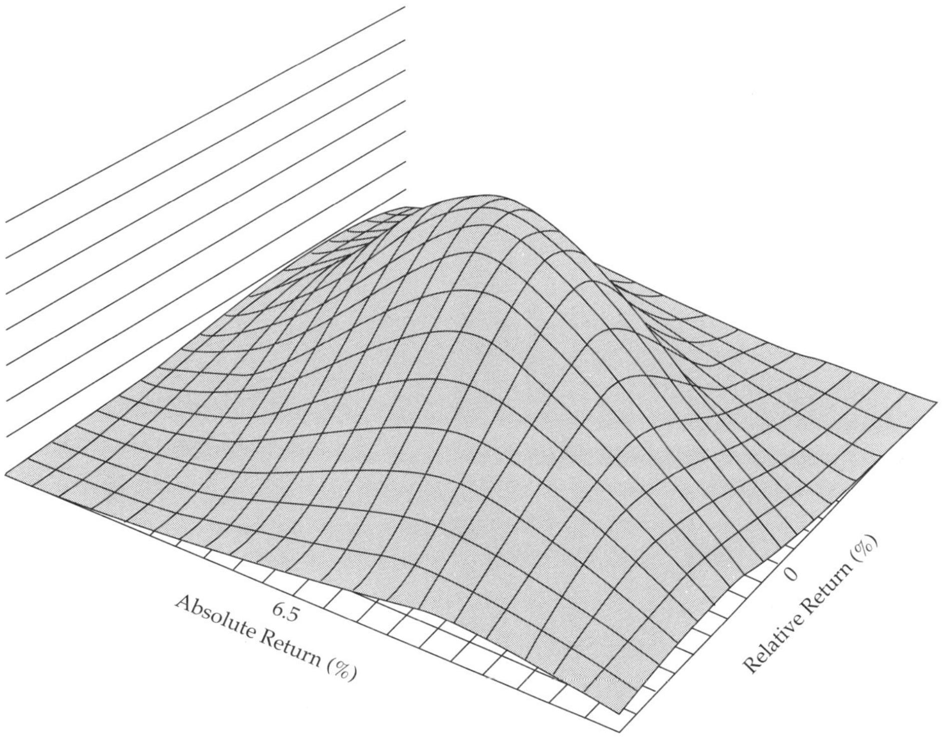

Figure 3. Probability of Absolute Failure

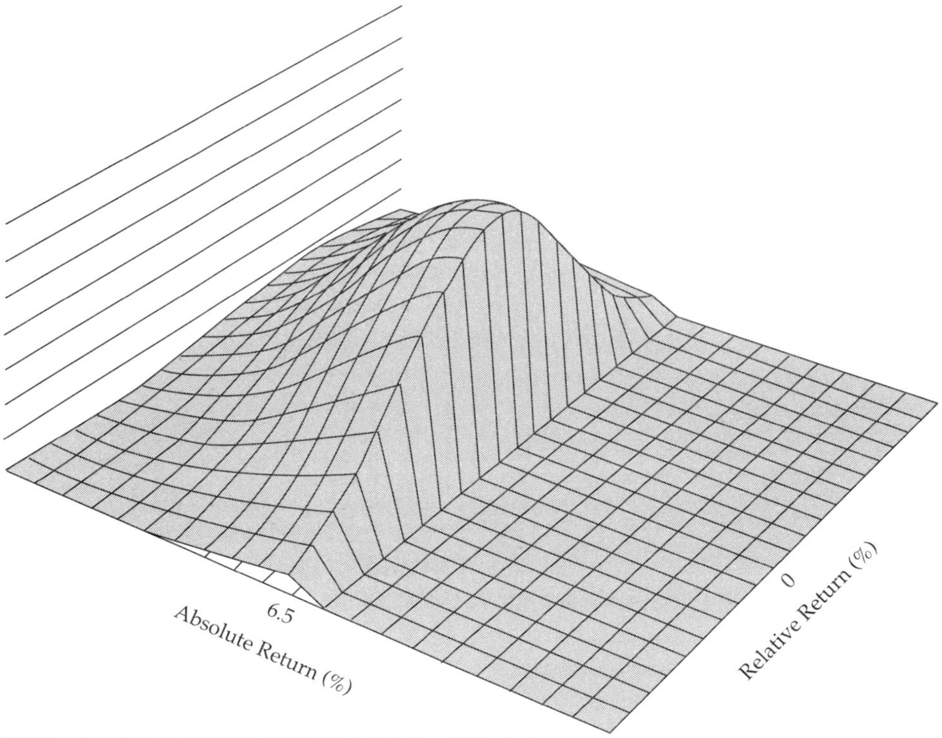

Figure 4. Probability of Relative Failure

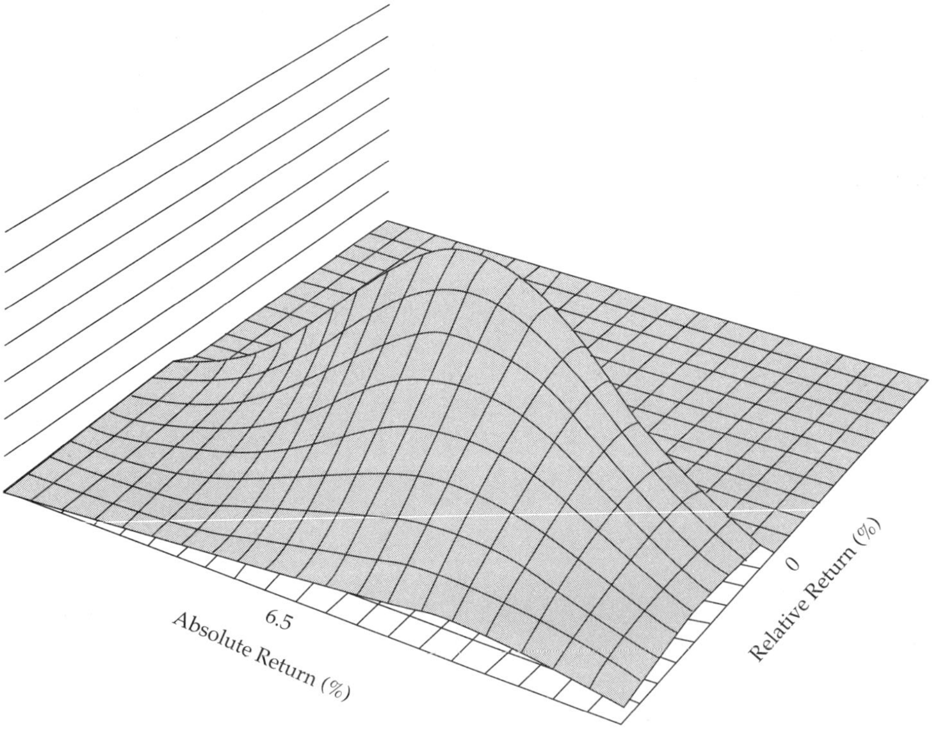

many portfolios with the same expected return but different combinations of standard deviation and tracking error. In an MVTE optimization, the investor would generate an iso-expected-return curve and analyze the available trade-offs. For example, to reduce tracking error by a certain number of basis

Figure 5. Probability of Concurrent Failure

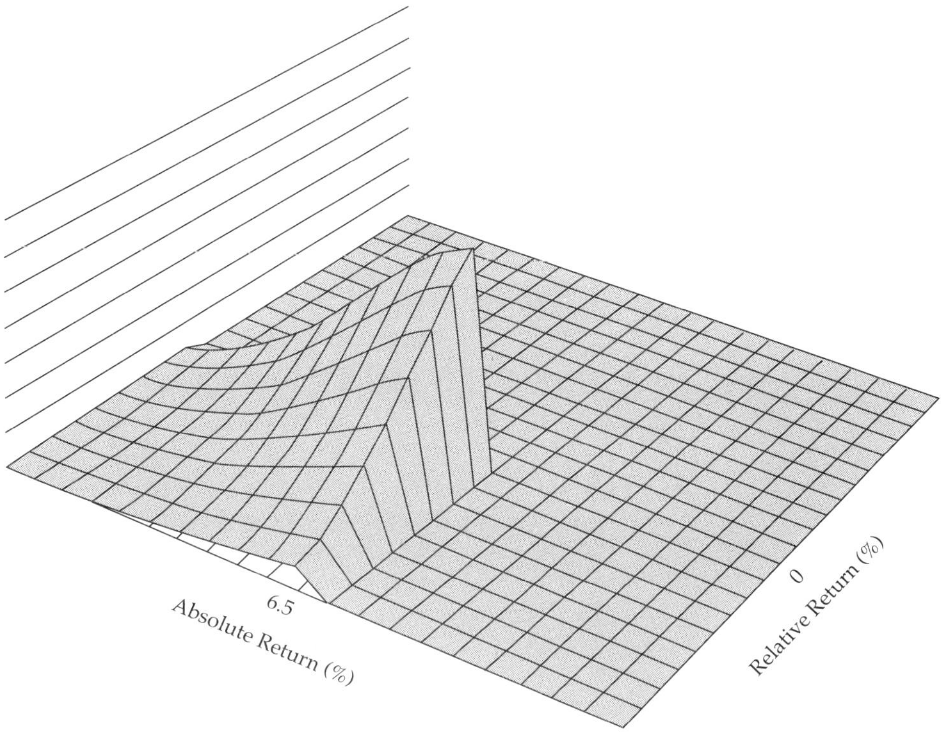

points, how much must volatility increase, or vice versa? Some region on this curve probably has both lower tracking error and lower volatility for the same expected return than a portfolio generated using constrained mean–variance analysis.

Mean–Variance versus MVTE Performance

A performance comparison of MVTE and constrained mean–variance optimization is provided in **Table 2**, which shows the currency returns, underlying country weights, expected returns, standard deviations of returns, and percentages of each currency hedged using both methods. Assuming no cross-hedging, the constrained mean–variance method produces a 10.62 percent expected return, a standard deviation of 13.38, and a 4.14 percent tracking error. Using MVTE optimization with cross hedging shows that, for the same expected return and a slightly lower standard deviation, tracking error is significantly reduced, by 73 basis points, to 3.41 percent. Such a reduction will be the case almost every time.

Table 2. Hedging Ratios: Mean–Variance Tracking-Error Method versus Constrained Mean–Variance Method

			Percent Hedged	
Country	Currency Return	Weight	Constrained Mean–Variance Method	MVTE Method
Canada	—	15.00%	—	—
United States	1.25%	25.00	0.00%	0.00%
United Kingdom	1.75	15.00	0.00	0.00
Germany	–0.75	10.00	10.00	0.00
Italy	1.00	10.00	0.00	0.00
Switzerland	–1.00	5.00	5.00	0.00
Japan	–2.00	20.00	20.00	26.44
Statistic		Underlying Portfolio	Mean–Variance Method	MVTE Method
Expected return		10.09%	10.62%	10.62%
Standard deviation		13.78	13.38	13.31
Tracking error			4.14	3.41

NONLINEAR CURRENCY-HEDGING STRATEGIES

The word "linear" applies to buy-and-hold strategies, or at least those that do not involve dynamically trading a portfolio. Although optimization is basically a static approach performed monthly, quarterly, or yearly, estimates are revised before each reoptimization. The word "nonlinear" refers to strategies that generate curved payoff functions; examples are option strategies, dynamic hedging strategies, or tactical asset allocation strategies. Nonlinear currency-hedging strategies include the use of traditional currency options, contingent currency options, or hybrid collars.

Traditional currency options. The typical nonlinear strategy for currency hedging involves buying an option. For a premium, a portfolio manager can protect a portfolio from currency losses beyond a prespecified threshold while preserving the potential to experience currency gains. Depending on the price of the option, of course, this strategy could be a nice trade-off. From a U.S. perspective, a one-year at-the-money option for one of the major currencies will cost about 3–4 percent of the portfolio, which may be too much for some investors.

Contingent currency options. An alternative strategy for people who are concerned about underperforming both the absolute and currency benchmarks involves engineering or purchasing a contingent currency option. This option protects a portfolio from currency losses beyond a prespecified threshold *only* when the portfolio's local return simultaneously falls below a prespecified hurdle value. This option is significantly less expensive than a traditional currency option, but the level of protection is also less. Investors are not protected when the underlying portfolio is doing well, but if they can tolerate currency losses when the underlying portfolio is doing well, this alternative might not be a bad one.

Hybrid collars. A hybrid collar provides protection against concurrent currency losses and portfolio losses in exchange for sacrificing currency gains when the portfolio's local returns exceed a prespecified threshold. Use of a hybrid collar does not involve an up-front payment for the contingent currency option but does require giving up currency gains whenever the underlying portfolio exceeds a certain threshold, which may appeal to many investors.

Relative Performance of Currency-Hedging Strategies

A comparison of the relative performance of a traditional currency option with a contingent currency option is provided in **Table 3**. Assume that options have a one-year horizon, initial values for the portfolio and the currency are 100, domestic and foreign interest rates are, respectively, 6 and 4 percent, portfolio volatility and currency volatility are, respectively, 12 percent and 10 percent, and portfolio and currency returns have zero correlation. In this example, the traditional option, with a floor equal to 100, eliminates any currency losses and costs 2.92 percent; that is, the investor must give up 2.92 percent of the portfolio's value for protection from currency losses.

If this option is conditioned on the portfolio falling below a hurdle equal to 100 (that is, the option pays off *only* when both the portfolio value *and* the currency value fall below 100), the price of the option decreases by a factor of 3, to 96 basis points—quite a difference.

What drives the value of this contingent option? The portfolio value, portfolio volatility, correlation, and hurdle value have nothing to do with the traditional option value, but they all affect the value of the contingent option. Despite changing some of these

Table 3. Traditional Currency Option versus Contingent Currency Option under Various Assumptions

Characteristic	Assumptions			
Portfolio value	100.00	100.00	100.00	100.00
Currency value	100.00	100.00	100.00	100.00
Horizon	1.00	1.00	1.00	1.00
Domestic rate	0.06	0.06	0.06	0.06
Foreign rate	0.04	0.04	0.04	0.04
Portfolio volatility	0.12	0.12	0.15	0.12
Currency volatility	0.10	0.10	0.10	0.10
Correlation	0.00	–0.10	0.00	0.00
Hurdle value	100.00	100.00	100.00	95.00
Strike price	100.00	100.00	100.00	100.00
Traditional option	2.92	2.92	2.92	2.92
Contingent option	0.96	0.83	1.09	0.56

assumptions, the price of a traditional option remains constant at 2.92. By first changing the correlation between the currency return and the portfolio return from 0 to –10 percent, the value of the contingent option decreases to 83 cents. That change makes sense, because as the correlation goes down, portfolio returns and currency returns are less likely to decline at the same time. By setting the correlation back to zero and increasing portfolio volatility to 15 percent, the value of the contingent option increases because higher volatility increases the likelihood that the option will end up in the money. Changing the hurdle value on the portfolio to 95 with portfolio volatility of 12 percent quite sharply decreases the option value. This strategy may particularly appeal to those who can tolerate currency losses when the underlying portfolio compensates with gains.

Although talking about these strategies and showing mathematical results is relatively easy, obtaining the option is another issue. I doubt a dealer would give these quotes, because the dealer has to bear the risk of implementing this strategy and will add a premium over and above the theoretical fair value of the option. Because the option prices are known, however, the option deltas are also known, so the option can be replicated by trading forward contracts.

The concept of the hybrid collar can be applied to currency risk versus portfolio risk as well as relative versus absolute risk. Assume an investor bears no credit risk by trading with an extremely creditworthy counterparty that guarantees the investor will not experience a currency loss whenever the portfolio has a return of less than zero. Think of a hybrid collar as an option that either will protect the investor from currency losses when the underlying portfolio performs poorly or will protect against experiencing simultaneous negative relative performance and negative absolute performance. In exchange for this protection, the investor will give up currency gains or relative performance whenever the underlying portfolio's value increases by some percentage.

The theoretical required portfolio return or hurdle rate at which an investor would be willing to give up currency gains in exchange for *never* simultaneously experiencing a currency loss and a loss in the portfolio depends on certain assumptions. **Table 4** provides theoretical hurdle rates for a hybrid collar using various assumptions about volatility, time horizon, portfolio floor value, interest rate, and correlation. For example, given portfolio volatility of 12 percent, currency volatility of 10 percent, uncorrelated currency and portfolio returns, a one-year horizon, and a floor of 100, the fair hurdle return is 15.4 percent, which must be appealing to managers willing to execute a hybrid collar at a 10 percent hurdle rate. So, in a perfectly efficient market, this collar should be accessible at a zero premium when the hurdle is set at 15.4 percent. The fair hurdle return increases when either the correlation or portfolio standard deviation is changed; for example, a correlation of –10 percent increases the hurdle rate to 15.8 percent, and an increase in portfolio volatility from 12 percent to 15 percent raises the fair hurdle rate to 16.9 percent. When the portfolio floor falls to 95, the hurdle return changes to 27.4 percent. Getting that kind of deal would require the ability to accurately forecast currency volatility, portfolio volatility, and the correlation between portfolio returns and currency returns.

Daily prices during the past 11 years for the Nikkei Index and Japanese yen were used to price this collar every quarter and then delta-hedge it by trading the Nikkei Index and the yen. The deltas were estimated from the previous quarters' standard deviations and correlations. The average error between the theoretical price and the replicated collar—2 cents on an index that has a value of about $16,000—is an extremely small error. Even in the worst and best cases, –16 cents and +68 cents, respectively, with what are obviously naive inputs for the parameters we have to estimate (currency volatility, index volatility, and correlation), the results are surprisingly close to the theoretically correct price. The reason may simply be that many errors offset one another—an error that drives the value one way is offset by another error that drives the value the other way—producing actual values close to theoretical prices.

Table 4. Hybrid Collar Hurdle Rates under Various Assumptions

Characteristic	Assumption			
Portfolio volatility	0.12	0.12	0.15	0.12
Currency volatility	0.10	0.10	0.10	0.10
Correlation	0.0	–0.1	0.0	0.0
Domestic rate	0.06	0.06	0.06	0.06
Foreign rate	0.04	0.04	0.04	0.04
Horizon (years)	1	1	1	1
Portfolio floor	100	100	100	95
Hurdle rate	0.1540	0.1583	0.1688	0.2740

CASH FLOW MANAGEMENT FOR CURRENCY-HEDGING STRATEGIES

One of the problems related to currency hedging occurs when a hedging policy or strategy works well, in the sense that the returns of the hedging strategy closely offset the experience of the currency exposure on the underlying assets. When currency returns are positive, losses on forward contracts are offset by gains on the underlying assets, but the gains are not accessible unless the assets are sold. Because we do not want to sell the assets in the portfolio every three to six months (depending on the expiration of our forward contracts), a method of anticipating the potential loss on the forward contract is helpful. So, within our optimization process, we segment the overlay component and do a value-at-risk analysis of the currency overlay portfolio.

For example, if a portfolio manager wants to be 99 percent confident that he or she will not have to liquidate assets in a portfolio to meet settlement requirements, how much will the manager need to have on hand in cash reserves? Depending on the maturity of the forward contracts, the required cash reserves can vary widely, as shown in **Figure 6** for a $100 million portfolio. Although this result is not particularly innovative, it has a lot of practical significance. The idea of estimating cash flow demands within a specified confidence interval has important implications for currency overlay portfolios. I encourage those who follow these hedging strategies to implement value-at-risk analyses.

CONCLUSION

Maximizing expected utility depends on the effect that currency exposure has on a portfolio's expected return and volatility. Although investors with long investment horizons might not want to hedge currency risk, investors' attitudes toward risk with respect to currencies should be consistent with their attitudes toward risk with respect to their underlying portfolios. Thus, investors should apply the same utility function to both the underlying portfolio and currency when they determine their hedging strategy for managing currency risk.

Global investors must understand how correlations affect minimum-risk hedge ratios. Almost never will the diversification between the currency and base-currency-denominated assets of a foreign portfolio be sufficient to overcome the volatility that currency exposure contributes to a portfolio. MVTE optimization almost always produces more-efficient results than constrained mean–variance analysis. Compared with sequentially optimizing the underlying portfolio and then the currency, MVTE optimization reduces volatility *and* tracking error for a given level of expected return.

Choosing the appropriate currency-hedging strategy requires determining the appropriate level of protection consistent with an investor's degree of risk aversion, assessing the costs and availability of different options, and evaluating each strategy against an appropriate benchmark—for example, evaluating a nonlinear strategy, such as a contingent currency option or hybrid collar, against a nonlinear or optionlike benchmark.

Figure 6. Cash Flow Management for Currency-Hedging Strategies

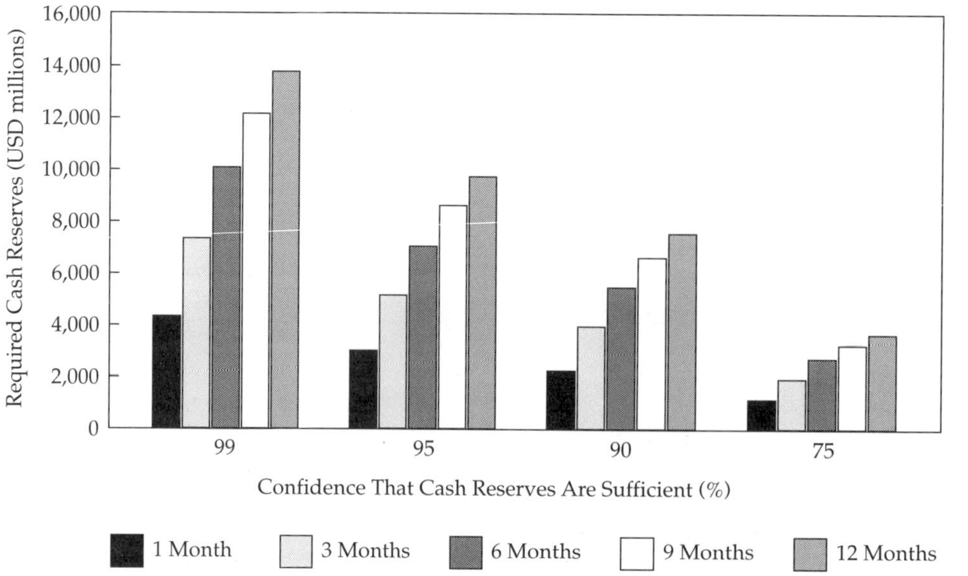

Question and Answer Session

Mark P. Kritzman, CFA

Question: If I am a long-term (five years plus) investor, why would I care about currency volatility measured over a shorter period?

Kritzman: I would agree with Froot (1993) that if you have a long horizon, and you measure your results in real rather than nominal returns, and real currency returns exhibit negative serial correlation, then hedging is counterproductive. One of the inconsistencies I have observed, however, is that people in the industry who hold this view do not apply it to the underlying portfolio. Their choice of the underlying portfolio often implies less tolerance for interim volatility.

An interesting exercise is to reverse-engineer the optimization process used to identify the underlying portfolio and back out the portfolio's implicit risk aversion. In other words, if you know the portfolio weights and have assumptions about returns, standard deviation, and correlation, you can reverse-engineer the optimizer to identify your degree of risk aversion. By risk aversion, I mean how many units of expected return you are willing to give up to reduce your portfolio's risk by one unit. That is the value you should use to determine the optimal hedging policy.

The enormous inconsistency is that the risk aversion implicit in the underlying portfolio is often much higher than the risk aversion implicit in the currency-hedging policy that people embrace.

Question: Please expand on when the hedging decision has to be made. In other words, should the portfolio allocation be made at the same time the hedging policy is decided or should those two processes be separate?

Kritzman: Constraints are bad. If you apply the process sequentially, you first go through an optimization to choose the underlying portfolio and then you worry about the currency exposure, but you have already effectively constrained the second optimization to hold a particular underlying portfolio. A more efficient approach is to solve simultaneously for the portfolio holdings and the hedge ratios.

The sequential approach is first to determine your underlying portfolio and then to introduce forward contracts to the optimizer and determine what your exposure to these forward contracts should be. To resolve both issues simultaneously, instead of optimizing among forward contracts, given an underlying portfolio, divide each foreign asset into two assets—a hedged asset and an unhedged asset. The expected returns of the forward contracts would determine the difference in the expected returns of the hedged and unhedged assets. Then, optimize in such a way that the optimizer may tell you that you want 25 percent of the portfolio in Japan unhedged and 25 percent in Japan hedged.

Question: What is the total exposure necessary before considering the hedging strategy?

Kritzman: This question introduces another inconsistency in the industry. In the U.S. experience during the floating-rate regime, U.S. domestic assets have been positively correlated with currency returns, particularly bonds. The intuition is that both bonds and currencies respond similarly to interest rate changes. That is, when interest rates go up, bond prices go down; the dollar typically will go up in a rising U.S. interest rate environment, so the currency return will go down. If that is the case, the mathematical result is that the smaller the percentage of the portfolio allocated to foreign investments, the greater the fraction you will end up hedging.

The inconsistency is that consultants will say not to worry about currency risk until you have 10–20 percent invested in foreign assets but they do not have the same attitude about how much of the portfolio ought to be allocated to a poor equity or bond manager. If a bond manager who has, say, 5 percent of the assets is doing poorly and is expected to continue to do poorly, the consultant will recommend firing that manager right away. Firing that manager will most often have a much less beneficial effect on the expected outcome of the portfolio than hedging a 5 percent currency exposure. The inconsistency is that although people are willing to ignore currency risk, which has a much bigger impact on the portfolio than does a particular manager's performance. For example, a U.S. investor who believes in the historical correlation between bonds and the German mark and does not have any investment in Germany should sell the mark against his or her bond portfolio and get the same expected return with less risk, thereby hedging the currency exposure of domestic assets.

Question: If one makes a decision to diversify in currencies, why should currency hedging be such an issue?

Kritzman: Maximizing expected utility depends on the effect currency exposure has on a portfolio's expected return and the diversification and volatility it brings to the portfolio. The net effect of all of these impacts determines whether or not to hedge; almost always, with respect to foreign assets, the volatility effect will overwhelm the diversification effect. In a situation in which you care about managing only risk, are agnostic about the direction of the currency, and want to maximize expected utility, you want to hedge.

Question: Would your reasoning change with respect to more-exotic currencies? Would you include additional factors for such currencies?

Kritzman: With exotic currencies, these results will be affected by market liquidity and the extent to which the exposure can be practically hedged. Take this factor into account when you estimate the net expected return of the currency forward contract. If the conclusion is still to hedge, you ought to hedge. My expectation is that some of the spreads in exotic currencies will imply that hedging the exposure would be too costly.

Question: If the payoff is asymmetrical, is the mean–variance method surely wrong because it assumes symmetry?

Kritzman: This question raises another in a long series of contradictions in the way we go about managing currency exposure. What puzzles me is that so many investors use a mean–variance optimization approach to construct their underlying portfolios. Use of this approach implies that they believe the return distributions of the portfolio are lognormally distributed. Not only is this belief a reasonable assumption and certainly what theory predicts but the samples we look at are reasonably consistent with that assumption. But use of this approach also implies that investors have concave utility functions. Many of these investors—who apparently have constant relative risk aversion, as demonstrated by their use of a mean–variance optimizer—choose either an option strategy or a dynamic trading strategy that generates some kind of skewed payoff function, a choice that implies they do *not* have constant relative risk aversion.

Investors seem to have different utility functions for different components of their portfolios. Both the currency and the asset components affect returns, and you should not care whether the return comes from the currency or the underlying portfolio because you should care only about return and risk. Managing currency exposure this way puzzles me.

If you are following a dynamic trading strategy to manage your currency exposure, you should measure that strategy against a benchmark such as purchasing an option or replicating an option. Using a linear benchmark to evaluate a nonlinear strategy is not helpful.

Question: Do agency theory and agency cost influence hedging practices, as in the university example?

Kritzman: The university example demonstrated how one can justify focusing on relative performance with economic considerations. Not being competitive will have economic consequences for the university. Economic considerations may also extend to corporate pension funds. To be more realistic, however, we are dealing with the utility function of the individual investor or investment committee that has a two- to three-year horizon. Tracking error becomes important, and agency issues drive the decision. We deal with agents as consumers of hedging strategies, so a lot of the strategies we develop recognize that reality.

Active Currency Management to Enhance Returns

Paul Day[1]
Investment Analyst
Quorum Capital Management Limited

Simple currency-management tools work reasonably well, especially when using several models reduces risk. Over the 1978–97 period, currencies with high interest rates, on average, did not decline in value by as much as their interest rate differentials. Although one would have experienced currency losses by investing in high-interest-rate short-term risk-free paper, the currency losses, on average, would have been more than offset by interest rate differentials. Thus, active management of currencies using convex payoff models or technical strategies—moving averages, gapping, momentum strategies, and filter rules—can enhance portfolio returns, but these strategies have downside risks.

After the breakdown of the Bretton Woods system in 1971, economists attempted, without any success, to forecast exchange rates. Two observations stand out in the last 25 years of floating exchange rates. First, high-interest-rate currencies, such as the British pound and the Italian lira, have tended to devalue by less than the difference between their interest rates and the average prevailing interest rates on core currencies, such as the Japanese yen, the German mark, and the U.S. dollar. Second, support exists for the hypothesis that currency returns trend.

Active managers need credible processes that are robust, not period specific and not dependent on outliers, to identify trends in the 20–25 years of current usable money market data and to take advantage of the forward rate bias. Data indicate that those countries with the highest average interest rates had the highest currency returns during this time period. Data also show that when the forward premium has been positive (negative) and when foreign interest rates have been lower (higher) than domestic interest rates, currency returns have been negative (positive). This finding suggests that active management of currency can enhance portfolio returns. Many tools—including the variance ratio, convex payoff models, moving averages, gapping, momentum strategies, and filter rules—are available to active currency managers to analyze and profit from potential currency trends.

This presentation provides a detailed discussion of how to use and interpret the results of the variance ratio with respect to trending, discusses several strategies for exploiting serial correlation in currency returns, and reviews the pitfalls and downside risks inherent in using these active currency management tools.

ECONOMICS

The modern paradigm for exchange rate movements began after the Bretton Woods system broke down in 1971. By about 1973, most major currencies floated against the dollar, and thereafter followed what Krugman (1993) describes as the "heroic age of exchange rate theory". Although few data were available at this point, quite a few theories developed, but economists quickly realized that their models did not work. Meese and Rogoff (1983) produced an importfant paper showing that the out-of-sample forecasting ability of most of these economic models was no better than the random walk model. Worse still, Frankel (1989) indicated that the very basic assumptions economists worked with in 1973 were either totally wrong or seriously flawed. The general view of economists in 1973 was that exchange rates would be as stable as the macroeconomic fundamentals underlying them. So, the funda-

[1]This written presentation was prepared with the help of D. Mark Tapley, CFA, managing director and chief investment officer, Quorum Capital Management.

mental view met with a lot of skepticism and had few disciples. For example, in April 1997, the Swiss franc was at 2.380 to the British pound; the year before, that rate was 1.828; the increase was more than 30 percent. Did the fundamentals change that much during this 12-month period?

WHAT NEXT?

These days, even avid fundamental model followers do not entirely want to go against a trend. Rosenberg (1993, 1996), for example, suggests a synthesis of technical and fundamental strategies. If we are cynical and abandon economics altogether, what have we got left? We have thrown away economic time series. Because floating exchange rates have prevailed, we are left to consider about 20–25 years of usable current money market data. We cannot refer to other periods, such as the brief time in the 1920s, when some rates floated. If these examples were relevant to the modern paradigm, presumably economists would not have been so wrong in 1973.

Many different events have transpired since 1973: the oil crisis; the growth of monetarism; German unification and its aftermath; periods of extremely high inflation, disinflation; and in the 1990s, severe asset-price deflation, for example, in Japan. The object is to look for simple anomalies (if any exist) in available money market data and develop them into robust investment processes that are not period specific, but the approach must be fairly credible and not dependent purely on outliers. After all, data mining by setting up 10,000 simulations in a black box and simply picking out the most significant or the best performing adds no value.

Annualized one-month returns on unhedged deposits between July 1978 and February 1997 are presented in **Figure 1**, in which the average annualized one-month interest rates of selected European countries are plotted against the average annualized return in U.S. dollars. According to the efficient market hypothesis, in the absence of a risk premium, all those points should lie on a horizontal line. Even ignoring the obvious outlier, the Swiss franc, the line of best fit through the rest has a positive slope, indicating *ex post* that those currencies with the highest average interest rates had the highest returns during this period.

The Forward Surprise

To compare current interest rates among European countries, **Table 1** shows the forward surprise on one-month forward contracts for a German investor. The forward surprise is the same as the forward return, and it is equal to the currency or spot return minus the forward premium; for example, the average annualized one-month forward surprise for British pound forward contracts is 2.4 percent. During the 1978–97 period, when the forward premium was positive—that is, when foreign interest rates were lower than the German interest rates—returns were negative. The Italian lira, for example, was never at a premium during this period, producing an average annual return of 2.6 percent. In Germany, when the forward premium was negative, returns were posi-

Figure 1. Unhedged Deposits: One-Month Currency Returns, July 31, 1978–February 28, 1997
(USD returns)

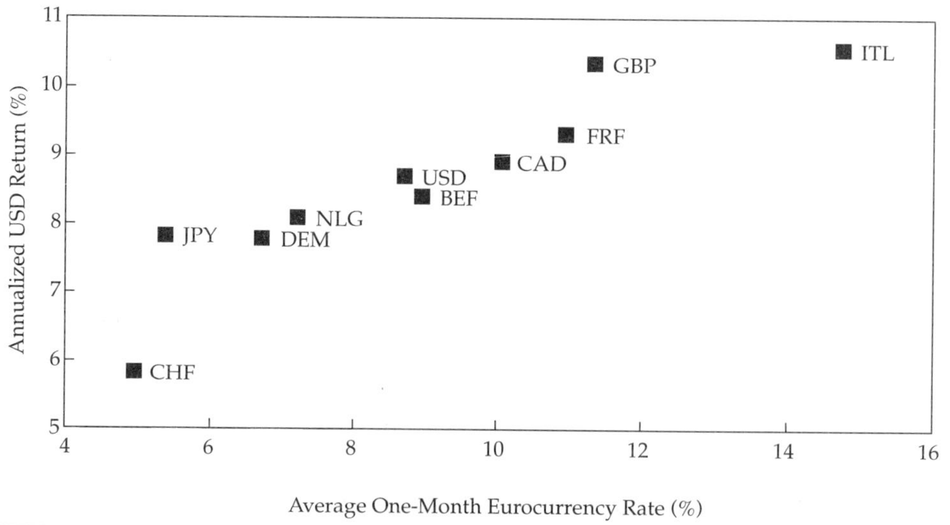

Table 1. Annualized Forward Surprise for a German Mark Investor, August 1978–February 1997

	Dollar	Yen	Pound	Swiss Franc	Lira
Average	1.0%	0.3%	2.4%	–2.0%	2.6%
Positive forward premium	–3.9	–5.9	–2.8	–3.0	—
Negative forward premium	2.3	12.1	3.3	11.3	2.6

tive. For example, the average annualized forward return for U.S. dollar forward contracts for a German investor was approximately 2.3 percent when the forward premium was negative. A simple strategy would be to sell those forwards at a premium and buy them at a discount—that is, go long the high-yield currencies and short the low-yield currencies. During the 1978–97 time period, following this strategy using equal weighting of these five currencies offered promise. The annualized return is 4 percent per annum, and the Sharpe ratio is about 0.8. The problem is that the worst one-year return was –14 percent until July 1993, and even over five years, the worst return was –13 percent.

The reason for this pattern is demonstrated in **Figure 2**, which shows forward returns for the Italian lira against the German mark. The worst single year is about –30 percent, but this strategy was an easy earner until about 1992, when a rather turbulent time ensued—a significant series of events following German reunification and the breakdown of monetary union. Since June 1995, another positive trend has been possibly developing.

The other well-known anomaly is the existence of trends in currency markets. The spot rate for the German mark against the dollar from slightly before the breakup of Bretton Woods to the present is shown in **Figure 3**. The spot rate trends down until about 1980, up until the mid-1980s, down until the late 1980s, and then in recent years, meanders. Although most people in the markets would say 1996 saw an upward trend for the dollar, that trend is obviously small in the big scheme of things.

THE VARIANCE RATIO

The variance ratio is a neat way of summarizing information on trends over a particular time horizon. For trends over four weeks, six weeks, or whatever, the variance ratio is defined as

$$\text{Variance ratio } (n) = \frac{\text{Var } (n \text{ period returns})}{n \text{ Var (One-period returns)}}.$$

For example, if $n = 2$, then

$$\frac{\text{Var}(r_{2t} + r_{2t-1})}{2\ \text{Var}(r_t)} = \frac{\text{Var}(r_{2t}) + \text{Var}(r_{2t-1}) + 2\ \text{Cov}(r_{2t}, r_{2t-1})}{2\ \text{Var}(r_t)}$$

$$\cong 1 + \text{Corr}(r_t, r_{t-1}).$$

The variance ratio is approximately 1 plus the correlation, which is the first autocorrelation coefficient. If one week's return is positively correlated with the next week, that would be a positive coefficient and the variance ratio would be greater than 1. If no relationship exists at all, the correlation coefficent will be zero and the variance ratio will be

Figure 2. Cumulative Forward Returns: ITL/DEM, December 1997–February 1997

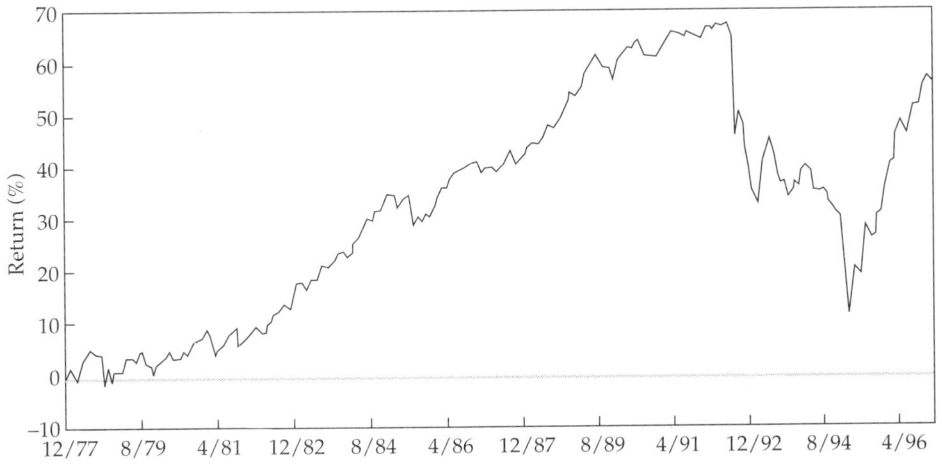

Figure 3. Qualitative Evidence of Trending: DEM/USD Spot Rate, 1969–96

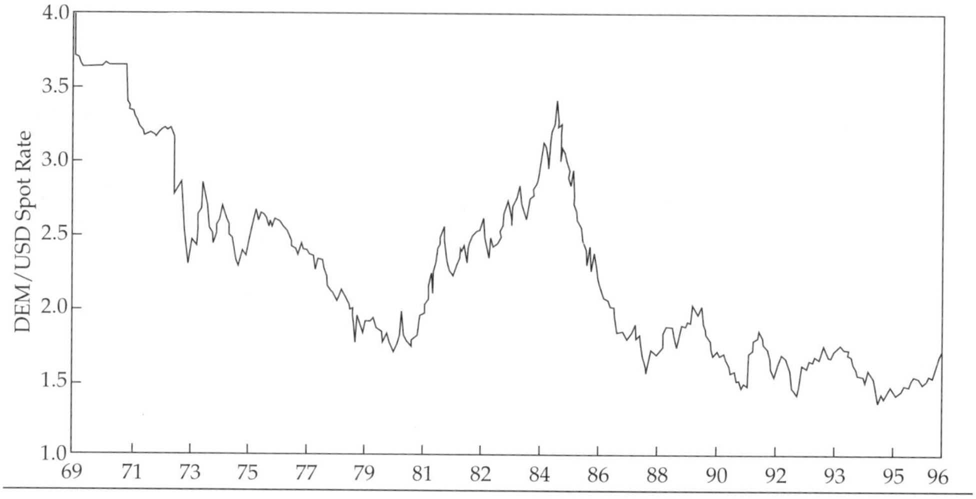

1. If mean reversion occurs over one-week periods, the correlation will be negative and the variance ratio will be less than 1.

The variance ratio applied to the DM/USD rate for the 1975–97 period is shown in **Figure 4**. This example uses weekly forward returns from the perspective of the German mark investor, but in this particular case, spot returns give something close to forward returns. On the x-axis is the number of weeks in the horizon, from 1 to about 200. The y-axis gives the variance ratio for the given number of weeks. The variance ratio starts off at 1 because the variance of one-week returns over one-week returns is simply 1. If the ratio is above the dotted line—and most of the time it is—it would be significant at the 97.5 percent level. After one week, however, the variance ratio is always greater than 1, implying some trend exists. This implication is not surprising because these ratios are based on the initial spot returns.

The significance of this method can be estimated using the Monte Carlo method, which is illustrated in **Figure 5.** The Monte Carlo method is used to determine the distribution of the variance ratio, given many different time series of returns. If the order of returns is not important, the Monte Carlo method shows whether the original variance ratio occurred as pure chance or as something significant that depended on the order. Levich and Thomas (1993a) used the same method to test the significance of trend-based trending methods.

The variance ratio is not period specific. For example, **Figure 6** shows a period that appears to have had significant trending—the dollar "bubble" and its subsequent burst in the mid- to late 1980s.

Figure 4. Variance Ratio for DEM/USD, 1975–97

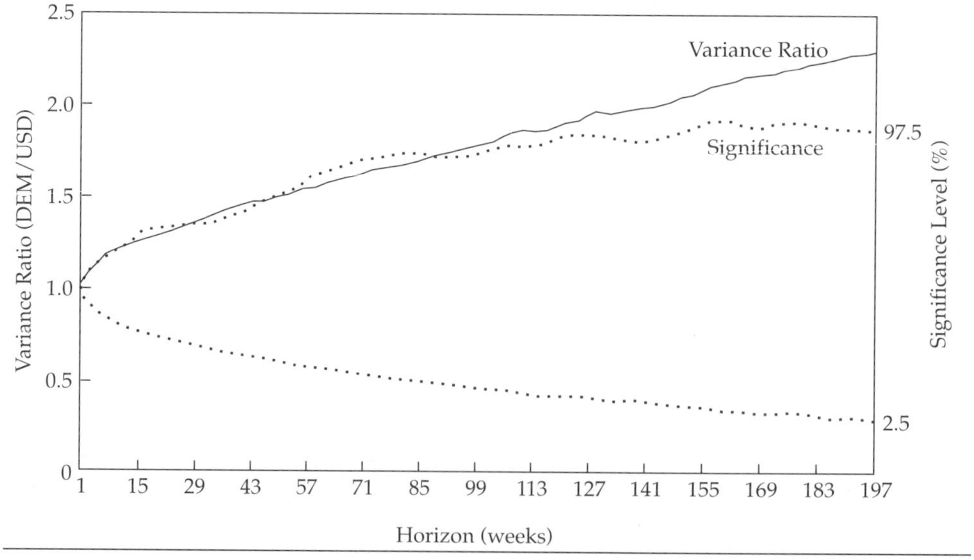

Figure 5. Variance Ratio Significance via Monte Carlo Method

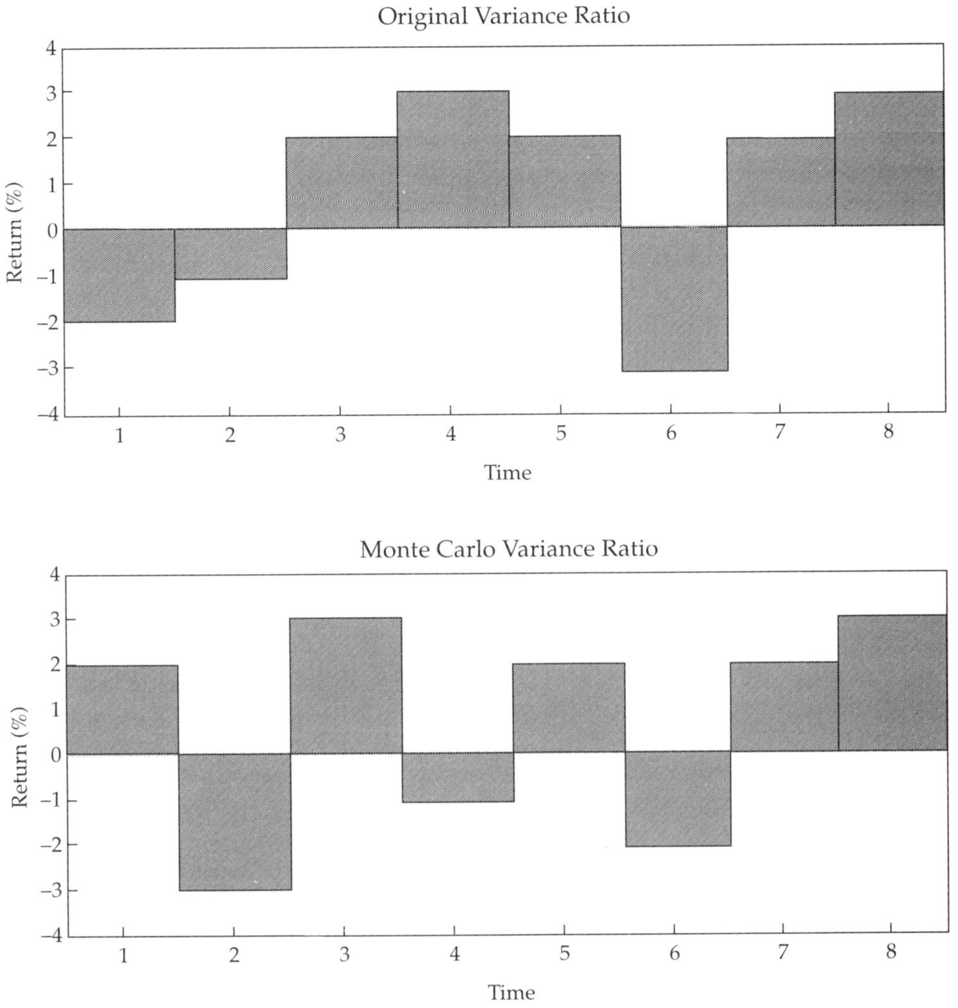

Figure 6. The Dollar "Bubble"

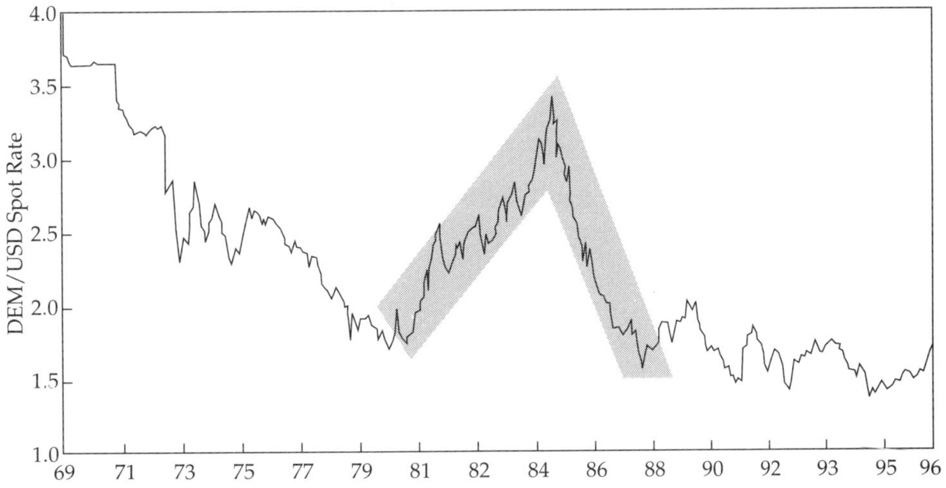

Figure 7. Variance Ratio: DEM/USD, 1980–88

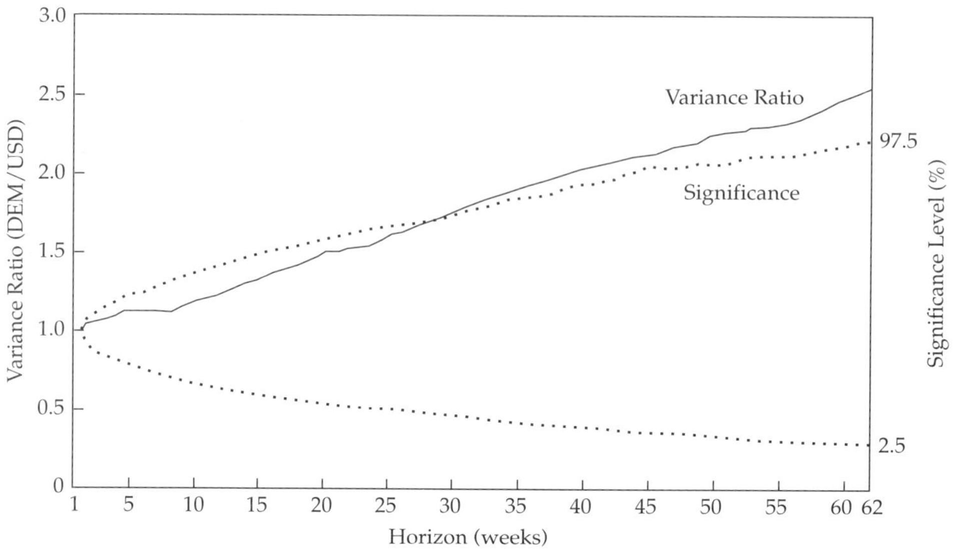

Although the time scale we examined is much smaller—about 60 weeks, **Figure 7** shows that the trend is still significant along all time horizons, with a little bit of noise from Week 2 to Week 13.

The variance ratio for the more stable period after the Louvre Accord in February 1987 is generally positive. Spot rates fluctuate during the January 1988 to February 1997 period, as shown in **Figure 8,** but the variance ratio, as shown in **Figure 9**, is positive for most of the range examined—up to about 80 weeks. Small trending occurs from Week 13 up to about Week 24, although that trending is not significant at the 95 percent confidence interval. The variance ratio more or less touches that level at about Week 13, but then it declines. For the longer horizon, the 52-week period, the variance ratio is approximately 1 and the situation is a random walk—significant at only a 50 percent confidence interval—and not a trend.

The variance ratio can be misleading, as the hypothetical example presented in **Figure 10** illustrates. Suppose an index time series resembles a sine curve around an underlying upward trend. The one-period returns are nonzero and nonequal, so although the variance might be small, it is certainly positive. This example has been engineered so that the variance of four-period returns—or multiples of four—is zero. The returns are constant, so the variance is zero over those time frames. The variance ratio for the $4n$ periods, therefore, is zero over something positive. Obviously, this example has a big underlying trend, but the variance ratio does not show it.

To summarize, the variance ratio is a useful first step to analyzing potential currency trends, but it has period-specific problems with capturing trends. It helps identify parameters for assessing the time scale of trends, but it carries a government health warning.

EXPLOITING SERIAL CORRELATION

Several models are available for identifying serial correlation, and not all are entirely independent—some hybrid models depend on more than one method. Classes of models include convex payoff models that involve option replication, or even buying options, and dynamic hedging; statistical time-series models; and well-known technical trading rules—double- and triple-moving-average methods, filter rules, momentum models, and the channel rule. All these models depend on the choice of parameters—volatility for option-based approaches, maybe correlation and time-period length for the double-moving-average approach.

Analysts normally choose the parameters for these models through optimization, using historical data in some way, although this method can be highly unstable. The problem lies with the functions analysts try to maximize, because a typical trading rule, such as the channel rule, has only one variable. Thus, maximizing returns over a given period depends on this one parameter. A detailed assessment of technical trading models in 1990 gave an example of the channel rule for the German mark in which the function is very erratic indeed.

Convex Payoff Models

Optimization of unstable, mean-reverting functions is always very dangerous. Diversifying among models reduces the risk of using volatile historical

Figure 8. DEM/USD Spot Rate after the Louvre Accord

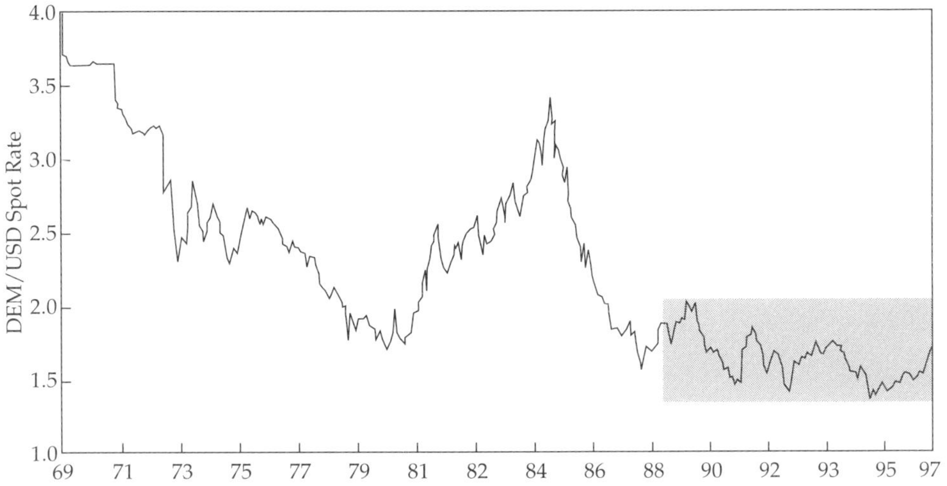

Figure 9. Variance Ratio: DEM/USD, 1988–97

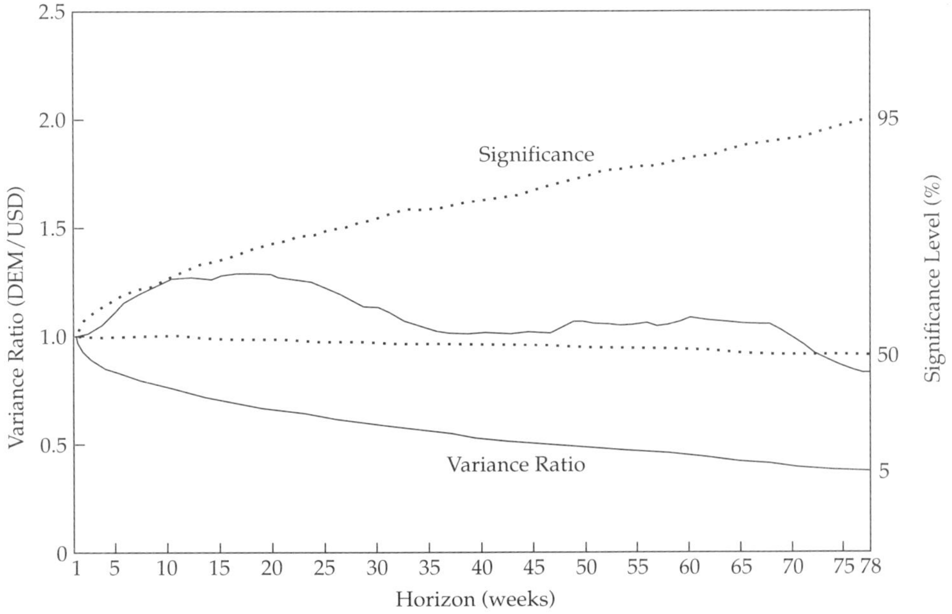

data, especially with technical models because of the parameter-setting risk. Using several different models avoids relying on only one model. We can also diversify among currencies.

Consider a convex payoff strategy, which is a buy-high/sell-low strategy. As shown in **Figure 11** for the mark/yen exchange rate, if the value of an asset increases and the parameters are set correctly, the asset is likely to increase in value over the next time period, so we should buy more of it, dynamically increasing our exposure. This strategy is similar to buying an option—a call, put, or straddle. Options can be replicated, but the problem is unknown forward volatility. We can lock in the volatility for an over-the-counter option because we know exactly how much we will pay in the beginning. But why adopt a convex payoff? Is buying an option always good? Certainly, we should buy an option only when we think it is cheap. What sort of options would our variance ratios suggest are cheap?

A reasonable strategy is depicted in **Figure 12**. A conservative German mark investor starting at the end of 1995 and going to mid-1996 cannot go long the German mark. This asymmetry is rather unpleasant for the investment manager who believes in trends, because a manager judged on absolute returns cannot go long the German mark. If judged relative to the option, this manager may do well. The danger is

Figure 10. A Problem with the Variance Ratio

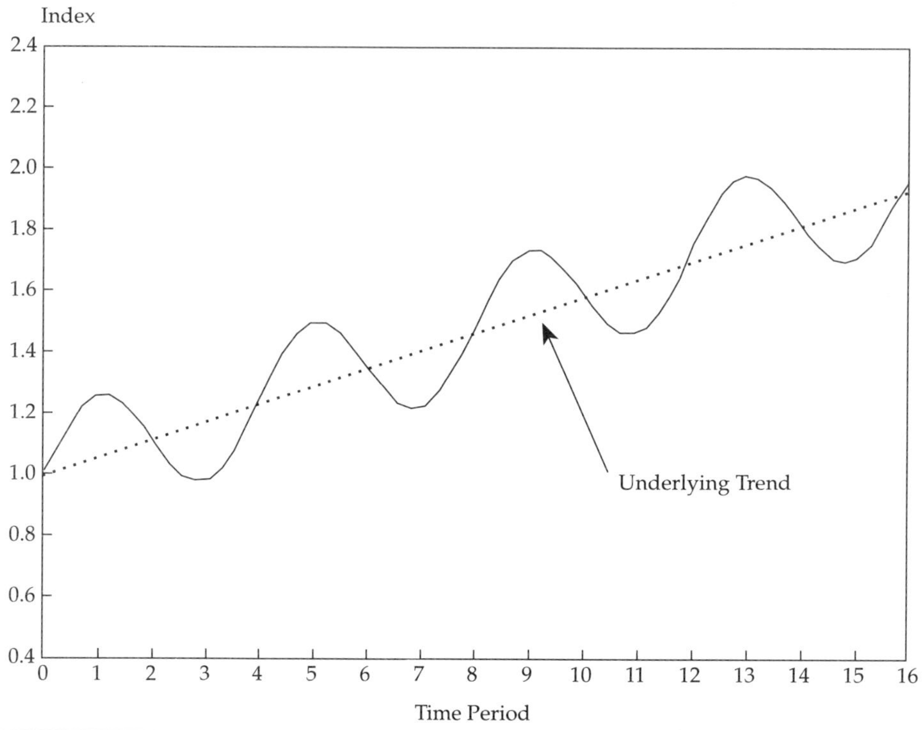

always present that the investor does not like the negative returns, so the conservative German mark investor will desire some protection and will have to pay some option premium. That investor will probably take some initial foreign exchange exposure. The investor can also begin with no foreign exchange exposure and gradually increase exposure, but this tactic is just a different option. The investor will always somehow have to pay for the options.

An investor could assess the likelihood of six-month trending by looking at average variance ratios. The pound sterling in 1992 had a strange period, so the investor would probably be a little cautious about sterling exposure and would start with only a 1.5 percent exposure in sterling and 3 percent exposure in the dollar and the yen. A nice strategy to pursue would be a structured trade-off between these competing currencies, which would give the investor almost an option on a basket of currencies. The position would be rebalanced every six months.

One argument in favor of dynamic hedging is that implied volatility is always too high, so the investor pays for the known certainty of payoff. Moreover, if an investor wants to exploit trending, the at-the-money implied-volatility curve for trending currencies always tends to increase, so 12-month options are more expensive than 1-month options. Exploiting the bought options can be difficult. In certain circumstances—for example, if EMU breakup is a concern—

Figure 11. Convex Payoffs and Option Replication

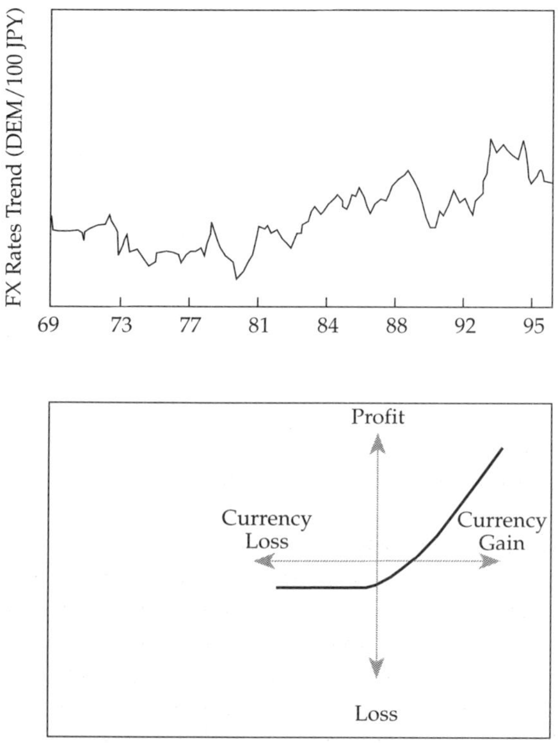

Figure 12. Cumulative Returns to Multicurrency Approach: Structured Trade-Off between Competing Currencies

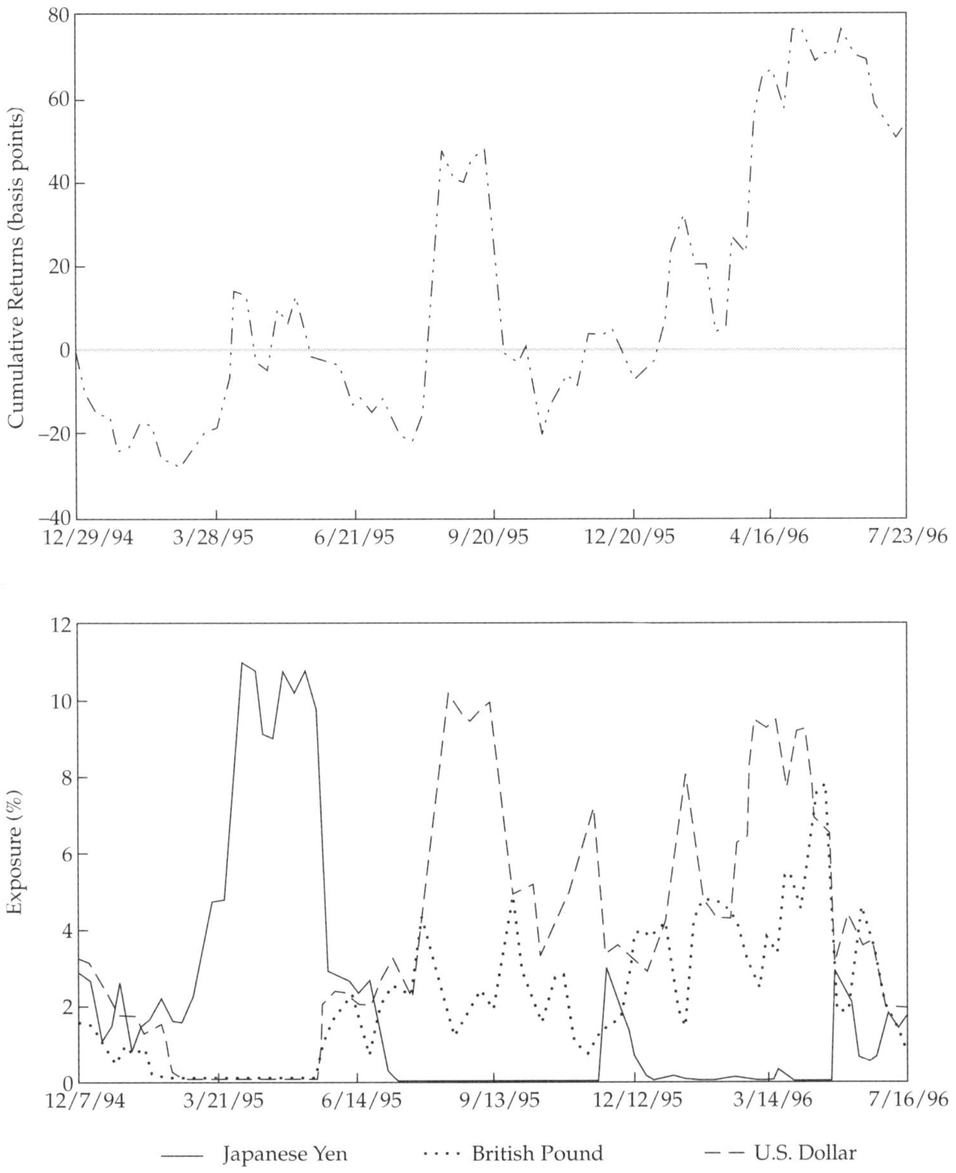

Note: Initial FX exposure: 1.5 percent GBP, 3.0 percent USD, and 3.0 JPY. Max FX exposure: 15 percent.

an investor may have to buy the options. If hedging is difficult and the investor is worried about gapping, an account-by-account basis works best.

Moving Averages

Technical models are often simply either long or short decisions, as shown in **Figure 13**. For the double-moving-average method, take two trends—a short-term and a long-term moving average. The short-term moving average places more weight on recent moves. If we believe in trends, we go long when the short-term moving average, either recent or trend, rises above the long-term moving average. Of course, to capture mean reversion, we go long when the long-term moving average rises above the short-term moving average. If the long-term moving average is 20 years or 100 years and the short-term moving average is one day, we recover nothing more than a purchasing power parity strategy, which makes this strategy more credible.

Two parameters can be very unstable, which is a problem. For example, between 1 and 100 days, an investor has about 5,000 different strategies to examine. So, the fact that some strategies will pay off in any given period is not surprising.

Figure 13. Double Moving Average: USD/GBP

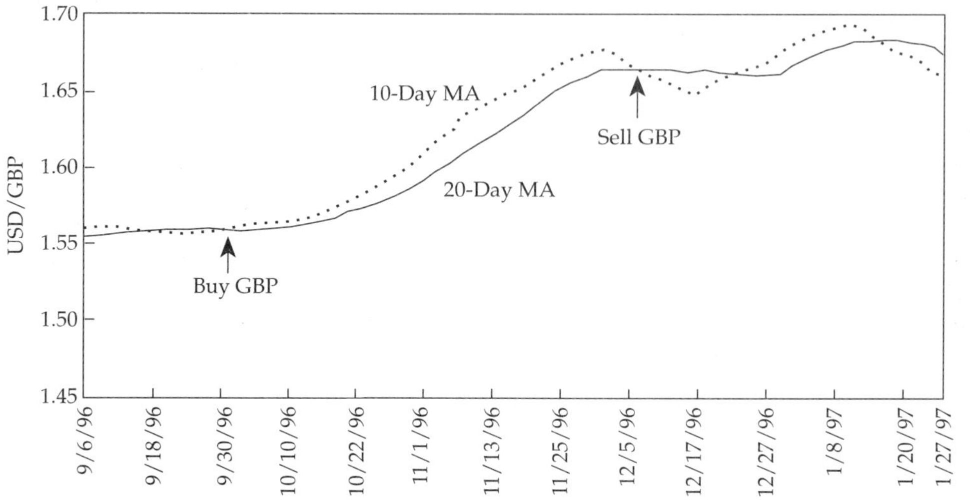

Gapping

For stepped returns, a gapping strategy can fail spectacularly and provide the worst possible returns. Gaps are a lack of price and volume information on a bar chart that should have price and volume information but the market activity is so great that the currency trades not at the expected level but at higher or lower levels. In a hypothetical example, returns might be 0 percent, 2 percent, 0 percent, and then 2 percent. The average return is 1 percent. Clearly, a trend exists, but if an investor selects, by historical estimation, a double moving average that looks only at the one-day moving average versus the two-day moving average, the investor will go long just after a rise of 2 percent. The next movement will be zero, so the investor will not get anything for that period. Then, the investor will go short, because zero is less than the one-day average, and lose 2 percent in the next period as the currency rises.

Filter Rules

Another technical trading rule with some credibility is the filter rule, illustrated in **Figure 14**. This approach uses only one parameter, the size of the filter. If exchange rates move *x* percent above a recent trough, the investor buys to capture the upward trend, and the investor sells when rates are *x* percent below a recent peak. The profit is the difference between the purchase price and the selling price. A small *x* captures the big trends earlier but may jump on false signals and get whipsawed—significantly.

Figure 14. Filter Rule: USD/GBP

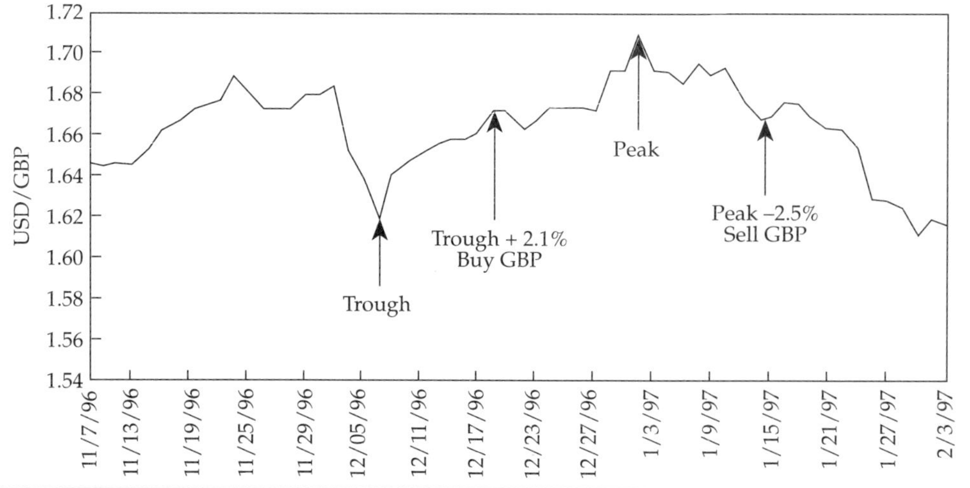

CONCLUSION

Although the biggest event to affect currency in recent times was Bretton Woods, if EMU comes about, the euro will perhaps be the next biggest paradigm shift. What will happen to trending after unification? The evidence of recent years involves three important currencies—the dollar, yen, and mark—and two important currency pairs—the dollar against the yen and the dollar against the mark. Some trending occurred in the dollar/mark pair, and noticeable trends occurred in the dollar/yen pair.

Current evidence suggests that trending will likely continue, but the long-term outlook for exchange rate targets is unclear until, for example, we know more about the direction of European central banks. Investment managers still need currency strategies, and the variance ratio is a useful statistic for developing one, although it does have period-specific problems. Other models, such as convex payoff models and technical trading rules, are available to the active currency manager to exploit serial correlation in currency returns and to enhance portfolio returns. Simple tools work reasonably well, especially when diversification among active management tools reduces risk.

The Role of Currency Overlay Managers

Ronald Layard-Liesching
Partner and Director of Research
Pareto Partners

Because many European funds are planning to expand rapidly into non-European investments, understanding how to manage foreign currency risk is crucial. Historical experience indicates that, over the long term, the value added after fees from a currency overlay program can be an additional 1–2 percent in annual return. Before implementing a currency overlay program, fund managers must realize the episodic nature of hedging return opportunities and have a detailed understanding of alternative overlay strategies.

Foreign currency risk introduces significant return volatility to international equity and bond portfolios. Although foreign currencies have no expected long-term return, large cumulative currency movements occur in relatively short periods of time. These movements provide opportunities for currency overlay managers to add value through risk reduction, return enhancement, or both. This discussion provides an overview of currency overlay programs, focuses on hedging and accounting issues, outlines alternative currency overlay strategies, and explains how to implement an effective currency overlay program.

HEDGING AND ACCOUNTING ISSUES

A clear definition of hedging is important to understand the intent of currency overlay programs. Hedging can be defined as the systematic reduction of preexisting, unmanaged price exposure. An immediate implication of this definition is that currency hedging never has the intent of increasing the existing currency-risk level. Creation of currency risk to seek return is not a form of currency hedging.

Another consequence of this definition of hedging is that the currency overlay manager is permitted to undertake only the net sale of foreign currencies. The overlay manager is not permitted to increase preexisting currency exposure by the net purchase of foreign currency. So, if a windfall gain results from a *rise* in foreign currency values, then any currency hedging will *reduce* this currency translation return. Plan sponsors must understand that hedging losses will occur in environments of translation gains, and vice versa, and that hedging losses are cash losses, whereas the offsetting currency translation gains are unrealized paper gains.

Return on an international equity investment has two components: the local currency equity return and the currency translation return (which may be positive or negative). For example, a European fund investing in the United States equity market will have returns from two separate sources: the rise in U.S. equity values in U.S. dollar terms and the movement in the dollar relative to the European base currency.

Currency as a Risk

International equity investments are generally undertaken to achieve greater diversification and higher equity returns relative to a domestic-only equity portfolio. Equity managers are hired to identify undervalued equities. A fund that invests capital in equities has a long-term horizon for expected returns, as confirmed by century-long studies of such returns. In contrast, currency is an exposure, not an investment, because no capital is invested to create the currency exposure—it is simply a side effect of the international investment decision.

Currency risk has no long-term horizon for expected returns. An index fund of foreign currencies may fluctuate a lot, but holding a currency exposure for a long period of time offers no expected return. Nonetheless, foreign currency exposure is obviously risky. So, a European pension fund investing outside Europe is faced with a large and unrewarded risk in the form of foreign currency exposure.

If foreign currency movements were small and/or averaged out over time, then active currency management would not be needed, but in fact, very large cumulative currency movements can occur in relatively short periods of time. For example, consider the Japanese yen movement during the past two years. For a European fund investing in non-European equity markets, nearly 50 percent of its total investment return (whether positive or negative) in a 12-month period will be accounted for by the currency translation returns. This situation explains why European funds that have large investments outside Europe have moved to appoint currency overlay managers to manage this otherwise unmanaged risk.

Accounting Issues

Because currency overlay is a hedging activity, the returns from the currency overlay program must be viewed together with the underlying currency translation gains/losses on international investments. The fund's net currency impact is determined by combining the currency translation return and the currency overlay hedging return as follows:

International equities return = Local currency equity return ± Net currency impact,

where

Net currency impact = Currency translation return ± Currency overlay return.

To illustrate how this accounting operates, **Table 1** shows examples of currency hedging with a weak base currency and with a strong base currency.

For a U.S. dollar-based fund investing in nondollar currencies during 1994, the dollar fell against those currencies by about 10.2 percent, which led to a windfall translation gain in the dollar value of the foreign equity holdings. Given such an environment, currency hedging, viewed in isolation, must cause a loss. In this particular case, the loss was roughly 2.9 percent. (The client had specified an unhedged benchmark and a loss limit of 3 percent.) With double-entry accounting, the net currency impact to the fund was a gain of 7.3 percent over this 12-month period. Note that the overlay loss was a cash loss but the translation gain was an unrealized paper gain. In this case, the loss of almost 3 percent was on a USD600 million total exposure, so close to USD18 million was paid in the hedging program. (The offsetting currency gain was about USD60 million.)

For a German-based fund investing in nonmark investments during 1994, the German mark was strong, so the fund had a translation loss of about 6.2 percent on its international investments. The currency overlay program offset those losses with currency overlay gains of roughly 4.1 percent. With double-entry accounting, the net currency impact for the fund was about –2 percent for the year.

Note that in both cases, the overlay return did not fully offset either the gain or the loss. Because the goal is for losses to be smaller than gains, value is added over time.

CURRENCY OVERLAY STRATEGIES

Two different philosophies are used in overlay management. One focuses on risk control; the other tries to time currency-market movements by using forecast indicators. The differences between these two philosophies lie in the objectives and also in beliefs about currency movements.

The difference in objectives is straightforward. The primary objective of a risk-controlling currency overlay style is to avoid currency losses relative to the benchmark; the second goal is to achieve currency returns—if any currency returns are available. In contrast, the primary objective of forecast-based approaches is to forecast returns in order to achieve returns and, secondarily, to control the risk of loss.

A risk-based approach is not necessarily right, and a forecast-based approach is not necessarily wrong, or vice versa. The choice of strategy depends on each particular fund's goals. Indeed, some funds will combine styles from the two different philosophies, and different styles are available within each philosophy of currency overlay management.

Forecast-Based Approaches

Three sources of information are used in forecasting currency returns: fundamental information, technical information, and market judgment. In the mid-1970s, virtually all currency managers looked solely at fundamental economic data, such as differences in price levels and current account balances between countries, as the basis for forecasting currency returns. Fundamentals do not change much from one quarter to the next, and thus since the early 1980s, no currency manager has used a purely fundamental style.

The other two sources of information are incorporated in the fundamental styles of today. Techni-

Table 1. Currency Hedging for a Weak Base Currency (U.S. Dollar) and a Strong Base Currency (German Mark), 1994

Currency Impact	U.S. Dollar Fund	German Mark Fund
Currency translation return	10.17	–6.17
Currency overlay return	–2.86	4.14
Net currency impact	7.31	–2.03

cal-based approaches process historical exchange return data to identify trends and overbought or oversold situations. Some overlay managers rely solely on technical data, and most of today's fundamental managers incorporate technical information in their process. Today's fundamental managers fall into two categories based on the way they use technical data. Some use a technical indicator, such as momentum, combined with other fundamental indicators. Other managers are fundamental "at extremes" and use technical models "in the middle."

The third source of information is market judgment. Analysts look at the flow of economic information but also at order flow in the markets and, in order to forecast currency movements, come to some judgment on likely central bank policy initiatives. Most of the forecast-based approaches incorporate some element of judgment, which makes determining how they may perform in the future difficult. The movement of managers, who make these judgment calls, between different currency overlay firms further complicates this situation.

Risk-Based Approaches

Three different approaches apply to risk-controlling currency overlay: currency-risk modeling, dynamic hedging, and the use of put options. Currency-risk modeling is Pareto Partner's proprietary approach to managing currency. It is based on a sophisticated five-parameter model of currency distributions. This approach contrasts with the Black–Scholes model, which uses one parameter and makes unrealistic assumptions of normal distributions and constant volatility (both of which are easily refutable for currency returns). Currency-risk modeling is not based on a risk-neutral theory; the positive expected return arises from a utility arbitrage. In simple terms, not all volatility is bad for a long-term investor.

Dynamic hedging takes a number of different forms. The most common form is known as synthetic option replication (essentially portfolio insurance applied to currencies). This form attempts to replicate the payoff of an option by the appropriate purchase and sale of currency forwards, with the hope of eliminating the markup that a bank selling an option would charge and reducing the time decay—theta—on the option. All the dynamic hedging approaches are price-rebalancing strategies: As the foreign currency price rises, the foreign currency is purchased; as the foreign currency price falls, the foreign currency is sold.

Some overlay managers use put options to hedge currency. Put options raise two major issues. First, they are derivative instruments (their price is derived from forward prices) and are purchased over the counter from counterparty banks. This course involves issues of liquidity, pricing, and counterparty monitoring. Second, purchasing options involves a cost. The currency options must be traded to try to recoup the substantial (3–4 percent) annual premiums. This trade involves forecasting changes in implied volatility.

Difference between Overlay Strategies

Forecast-based currency overlay styles differ fundamentally from risk-controlling currency overlay styles. This distinction is best understood by examining the structure of the currency market, which is by far the largest financial market in the world.

The latest studies by the Bank for International Settlements show currency turnover of USD1.2 trillion a day, 80 percent of which is in only eight currencies. In other words, as of April 1995, eight currencies accounted for USD1 trillion of turnover a day, and current volume is more than 30 percent above this level. Compare this turnover with the turnover of the equity markets. For all North American stock markets, annual turnover in 1995 was USD5.7 trillion. The USD1 trillion of *daily* currency turnover covered eight different currencies; the USD5.7 trillion of *annual* stock market turnover covered more than 4,000 different shares.

Not only is the currency market much more liquid than the other markets, but all the information of a fundamental and a technical nature is freely available to all the participants, fulfilling on paper all the conditions of an efficient market.

One feature of efficient markets is that forecasting future movements based on publicly available information should not be possible. The degree to which foreign exchange rates can be forecast has been extensively studied by academics worldwide. Meese and Rogoff (1983) conducted a widely quoted study on this topic and found that even when future fundamental variables are known, forecasting future exchange rates is impossible. When the Meese and Rogoff paper was published, it created enormous controversy because it appeared to contradict common sense. In the ensuing 14 years, many attempts have been made to find currency-forecasting models that outperform tossing a coin. The first study that beat the random walk over a two-year period using fundamental information failed, like all others, to beat tossing a coin in a period shorter than two years.

Note that the academic results on currency forecasting relate only to public domain research. Forecast-based currency overlay managers use proprietary approaches in forecasting currency returns. Fundamental data can be of value in indicating the direction of possible currency movements, but such information is not consistent and has little size information. We and other currency managers use overlay styles based on risk control rather than forecasting currency returns, because the belief that risk can be forecast in the short run does have enormous academic support.

Currency Overlay Payoffs

The real difference between the forecast-based and risk-controlling philosophies of currency management is the return payoffs they offer. **Figure 1** and **Figure 2**, respectively, show simulated payoff patterns for successful and unsuccessful applications of the forecast-based and risk-controlling overlay styles. Note that if a particular forecast-based style is successful, it can provide substantially higher returns than a risk-controlling approach in the short run. The potential for higher return, however, comes at the cost of potentially poor risk control, resulting in substantially negative interim outcomes.

People used to argue that a return-forecasting style must be used to add value, but this argument is not true. In the short run (less than one year), the highest-performing currency manager will almost always be one using a forecast-based style, but the top-performing manager is likely to be different from year to year. For example, one fundamental manager took excellent intra-European currency positions in

Figure 1. Payoff for the German Mark Using Forecast-Based Style

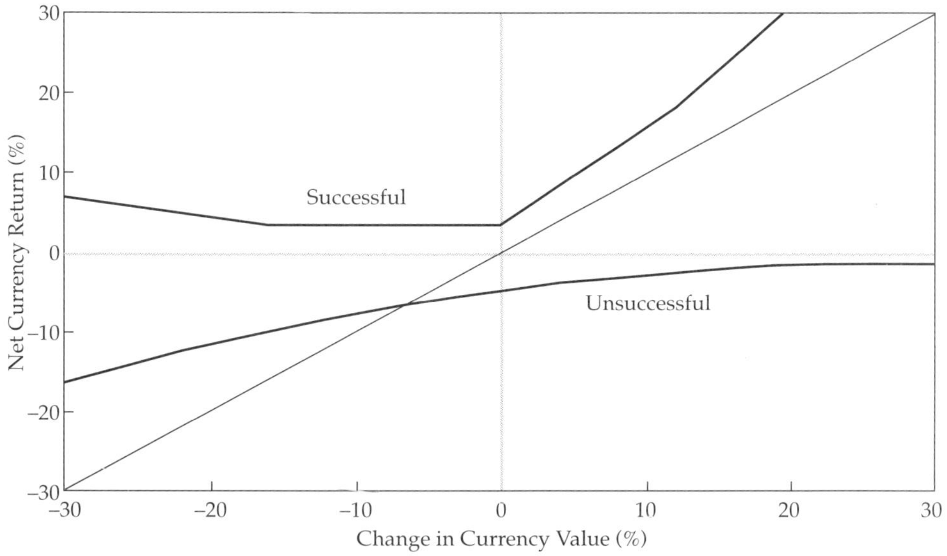

Figure 2. Payoff for the German Mark Using Risk-Controlling Style

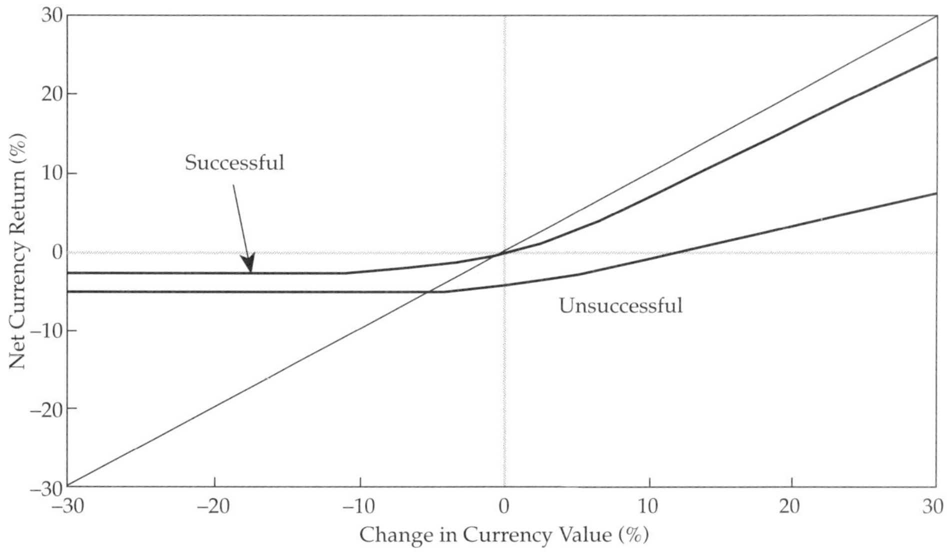

1990, one technical manager had strong performance in 1992, a judgmental manager had good performance in 1993, and so forth. So, examining long-term (at least three years) returns for all clients is important.

Adding Value in Currency Overlay

Discussion of currency overlay always starts *after* the international investment decision. Funds do not decide to expose their fund to foreign currency and hire a currency overlay manager. A fund will decide to invest capital internationally and then address the currency exposure.

Currency overlay adds value in all environments by reducing the fund's currency risk: It permits the international allocation to be expanded safely and rapidly (most large funds are now targeting a total international commitment of 30 percent of total assets). Reduction in volatility—particularly downside volatility—is attractive. Funds, however, hire active overlay managers to add value as well.

Viewed purely in isolation, an overlay will reduce windfall currency gains when the base currency weakens. For example, **Figure 3** shows the currency translation swings for a U.S. dollar-based fund in 1994; it does not show the return on the underlying equity investment of the fund. During that year, the dollar fell as the foreign currencies rose. This fund had selected an unhedged benchmark and specified a maximum tolerance of 3 percent performance of this benchmark. At the end of the 12-month period, the fund had a 10.2 percent translation gain but close to a 2.9 percent overlay loss, resulting in a net currency gain of 7.3 percent. When the base currency is weak, a strict hedging mandate does not permit the overlay manager to buy the rising foreign currencies, because this move would increase pre-existing currency exposure.

Figure 4 illustrates how a German mark-based fund with investments in the United States fell in value as the dollar declined against the mark. For a strong base currency, with the foreign currencies falling, currency overlay offsets the currency translation losses. In this particular 12-month period (the benchmark was again unhedged, with a 3 percent loss limit), the overlay hedging process had an opportunity to add value: An overlay gain of 4.1 percent partly offset the –6.2 percent translation loss, resulting in a net currency return of about –2 percent.

The opportunity to add value comes when, and if, the base currency strengthens. For example, **Figure 5** highlights the total value added for a U.S. dollar fund in 1996, when the dollar strengthened sharply, particularly against the yen. Of course, the rise in the dollar had exactly the opposite effect on the European fund. With the U.S. dollar rising, a European fund has no opportunity to hedge (sell dollars) and add value. The key goal is to hold on to the already-achieved returns.

In summary, currency overlay adds value both by reducing risk and by increasing fund return, although the opportunities to add value in currency management do not occur every year. The *episodic* nature of hedging return opportunities is one of the aspects of overlay that makes it difficult for the nonexpert to understand. Lay investors are used to investing capital with at least the hope of outperforming passive benchmarks every year. This hope is not the case in currency overlay, which can have years of zero return, years of small negative return, or even periods that have a high positive return.

Figure 3. Currency Translation Swings: U.S. Dollar Fund, 1994

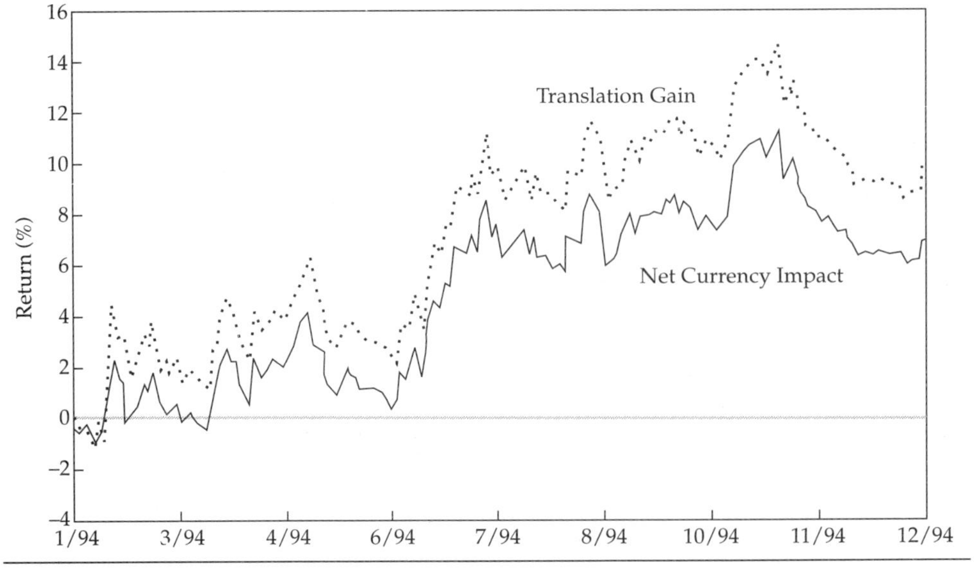

Figure 4. Currency Translation Swings: German Mark Fund, 1994

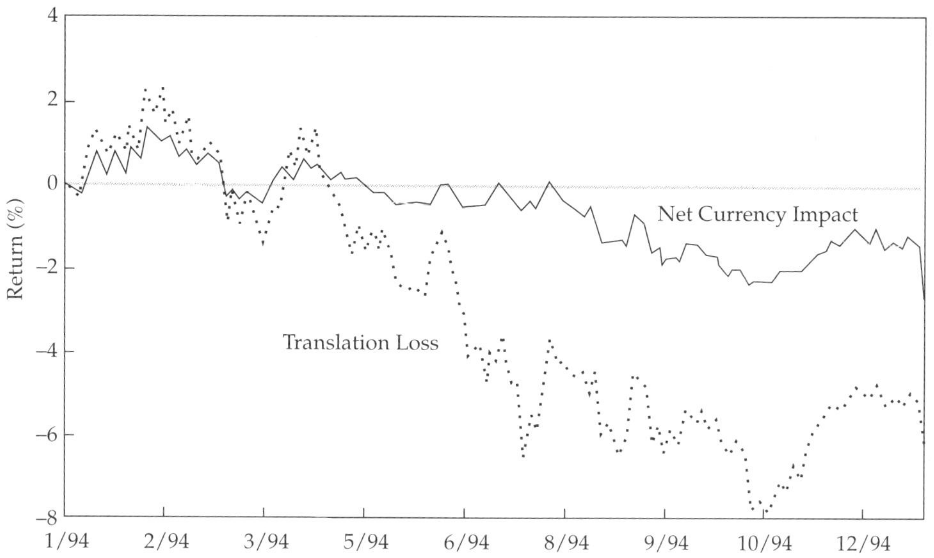

Figure 5. Currency Translation Swings: U.S. Dollar Fund, 1994–96

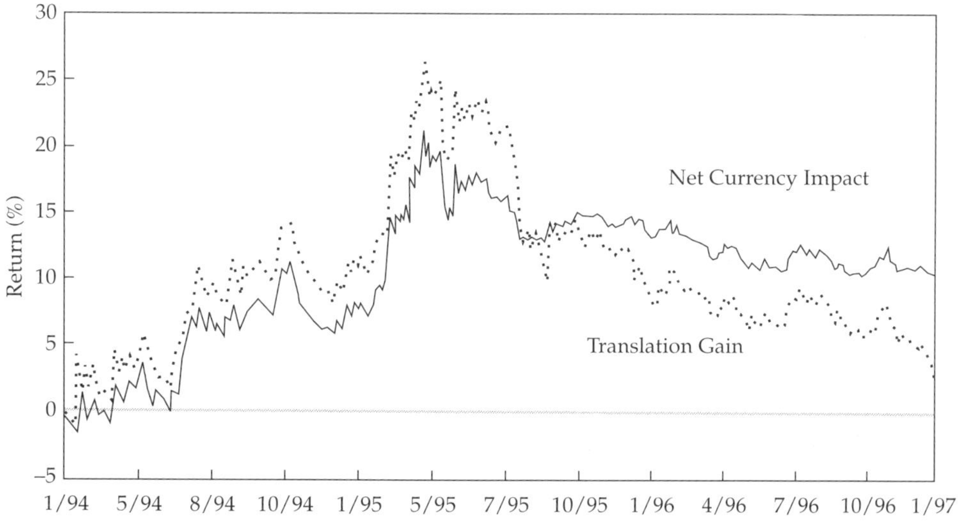

IMPLEMENTATION

Before undertaking a currency overlay program, a fund must develop clearly specified goals for the program, because different funds can legitimately have different goals for managing their currency exposure. Many of the large funds start by building their international exposure while controlling currency risk, so they often start their currency-management experience with a core risk-controlling style. Other funds (particularly those that are well funded and have small international exposure) may choose a more return-oriented approach and may view currency management as a way to enhance international returns.

The development of a consensus within a fund on the relative goals of currency management—protecting assets versus enhancing return—is critical, but a fund's style often evolves. For example, a manager that wishes to aggressively build international exposure may start off with a cautious approach to currency simply to avoid adverse currency outcomes that could derail the international investment program, but this fund could later become more adventurous. We have also seen the reverse: funds moving to a risk-controlling approach after first trying return-seeking approaches.

Once appointed, a currency overlay manager operates with total independence from the underlying international equity or bond managers. All the currency overlay manager needs to know is the currency allocation of the underlying managers and the instruments they hold. This information is usually obtained monthly, or more frequently if market conditions warrant, and it is available from the reports the global custodian provides (if a global custodian is used). Alternatively, the currency allocation may be provided either by the pension fund or, in some cases, directly by the fund managers themselves. When an index fund is overlayed, the exact daily allocation is known.

The currency overlay manager needs to know whether the underlying investments are in equities or in bonds in order to ensure that the best estimate of the underlying asset values is continuously available. For example, during the Exchange Rate Mechanism crisis of 1992, overlay managers fully currency hedged their clients' investments in U.K. equities. During the week prior to the British pound crisis, the U.K. equity market also fell sharply, so reducing the currency hedge size to reflect the decline in the underlying value of the actual investments was important.

Hedging Instruments

Currency overlay managers generally hedge by using currency forwards. A few currency overlay managers also use currency options for hedging purposes. Currency options are derivative instruments—their price is derived from currency forwards—and using these options requires special care. The currency overlay manager, acting as agent, will take currency positions on behalf of the fund to reduce the fund's exposure to foreign currencies. The overlay manager will, for example, instruct a bank to sell the Japanese yen versus the base currency on behalf of the fund, which reduces the fund's exposure to a fall in the yen relative to the base currency. This activity results in a foreign exchange forward contract. No money is exchanged at the inception of the contract, but at its final maturity, either the bank will send a check to the fund or the fund will send a check to the bank. A gain (cash coming to the fund) will be realized if the foreign currencies fall, and a loss (cash sent from the fund to the bank) will be realized if the foreign currency rises. Note that the transaction is directly between the fund and the bank. The currency overlay manager acts as an agent, not as a principal, in this transaction. To undertake these transactions, proper documentation is established between the fund and the foreign exchange bank, together with documentary authorization of the role of the currency overlay manager.

Performance Measurement

On a monthly basis, the currency overlay manager will measure the unhedged currency translation gains or losses and the currency overlay returns and also compare performance relative to a fully hedged benchmark. Because currency exchange rate data are readily available, the performance the overlay manager reports can be easily verified by a third-party audit.

Comparing returns between different currency overlay approaches is extremely difficult because of differences in benchmarks, in base currency, and in the starting point of the programs. Most of the major currency overlay managers, however, have been appointed jointly by at least one fund, and in these cases, the result of one approach can be directly compared with that of another.

Costs of Currency Management

The currency market trades 24 hours a day, unlike equities markets, which generally trade only for 6 to 8 hours. The currency overlay manager must monitor the hedges on a 24-hour basis in case large currency movements develop. Although the concentration of currency movements is not generally known in advance, the entire currency movement during a year is often concentrated in less than 5 percent of the days in the year. Thus, continuous monitoring makes running a currency overlay service expensive for a portfolio manager.

Eighty percent of currency trading occurs in the European time zone, so many currency overlay managers are based in that time zone. Because of the cost of running currency overlay services, overlay managers are relatively scarce; approximately 12 are available to large pension plans. More than half the currency managers use forecast-based approaches to currency overlay; the others offer risk-controlling styles. Portfolio managers and fund directors often use investment consultants, some of whom are highly knowledgeable about currency overlay activities, to evaluate the relative merits of different currency overlay managers.

The fees for currency overlay services are based on the size of the account, with fees typically ranging down from 35 basis points. Currency overlay managers can also be hired on a performance-fee basis, but care must be taken to ensure that the currency manager does not assume excessive risk.

CONCLUSION

Currency overlay, used by global pension funds for the past eight years, is a complex activity. Because a fund's staff may need many months to evaluate the issues involved, currency overlay should be considered only when the nondomestic currency exposure is significant or will become significant. Once the nondomestic exposure of a fund is significant (either in percentage of total assets or simply in amount of currency), currency swings will have a material effect on a fund's total return.

Three conclusions can safely be drawn from currency overlay experience. First, currency overlay returns are episodic—that is, they cannot be positive every year. Second, over the long term (three to five years), value added after fees can be around 1–2 percent annually. Third, currency overlay substantially reduces a fund's pre-existing currency risk. The reduction in currency risk is the most critical part of currency overlay work, because as currency risk declines, increasing the international allocation becomes much safer. This risk reduction is particularly important for European funds, many of which are planning to expand rapidly into non-European investments.

Question and Answer Session

Ronald Layard-Liesching

Question: Why are currency-management fees so low compared with the total return potential?

Layard-Liesching: The question also probably relates to the "currency as an asset class" strategy. This strategy is a totally separate activity in which people show, for example, 14 percent rates of return. Currency overlay yields only 1–2 percent a year with no leverage. You never go long and short; you are only going short. For the currency-as-an-asset-class managers, the fee structure is 200 basis points a year and 20 percent of the profits. These fees are extremely high for those people who claim to be able to time currencies. In my 25-year career in managing currencies, I have observed that those people do not have long careers. They have to charge high fees because they will probably not be around in the long term.

The fees for hedging, however, are very well established and are monitored by consultants, such as the Frank Russell Company. Currency managers are in two groups: the currency speculators, who are a continually refreshed pool and who charge exorbitant fees, and the currency overlay managers, who will be around for long periods of time and who charge modest fees.

Question: What do you think about currency overlay programs for emerging markets?

Layard-Liesching: Emerging markets should be excluded from currency overlay programs, because by the time you need to hedge, there is no forward market. We conducted a study in mid-1994 analyzing the link between the emerging stock markets and currency movements. The results show that within two years after a major devaluation takes place in an emerging market, the equity market will go up by more than an offsetting amount in U.S. dollar terms. For a European investor, the emerging market currency exposure is strategically a U.S. dollar exposure, because people in emerging markets are selling dollar-priced goods, so if they devalue, the value of the shares will tend to go up. This situation is not true for developed countries.

Question: In light of the restructuring of the currency systems, how do you see currency overlay strategies developing during the coming years, especially in terms of prevailing styles?

Layard-Liesching: We have been surprised by the pace with which continental European firms have embraced currency overlay management as a result of their internationalization. They have moved from portfolios that five years ago might have been 95 percent bonds into substantial international portfolios, and by international, they do not mean European—they mean Japan and the United States. Because currency is a large part of the return, they are moving ahead fairly rapidly to look at the different currency overlay styles.

Question: What will the elimination of some of the trading currencies in the European concentration imply for your diversification strategy and attitude toward currency overlay strategies?

Layard-Liesching: People outside and inside Europe are looking at Europe and saying, "Irrespective of whether monetary union comes about, a convergence of policies and markets is taking place." London is emerging as a major European financial center, which reduces diversification opportunities. U.S. funds want to move out of Europe because it is now one market, and continental European funds want to increase aggressively their allocation to emerging markets, the United States, and the South Pacific Basin for the same reason. Thus, we doubt that the EMU is going to reduce currency movements between the blocks, but we hope it will reduce movements within the block.

Question: Because your use of risk control implies a forecast of unacceptable risk in order to generate an action, can it be considered forecast free?

Layard-Liesching: If you're asking how we can add value with risk control, the answer goes to the heart of theory. I will not go into detailed mathematics, but when we talk about a forecast, the idea of a distribution is always present. Suppose we forecast that the yen is going to 130: Do we mean 130 or 135 or 128?

Academic research, notably by Meese and Rogoff (1983), found the startling result that even if you know next year's inflation, interest rates, and current account balances, you cannot forecast currencies any better than tossing a coin. This result was so surprising that Meese thought it might be attributable to interest rate effects, but he found that such was not the case; the evidence shows that forecasting cannot beat tossing a coin over a two-year period. (Obviously, other currency managers' models are not in the public domain, but we find no support for the ability to forecast currency returns consistently.) The distribution has other aspects—for example, volatility, which is technically the second moment of the distribution.

In one sense, we are forecasting, but we are not forecasting the first moment of the distribution. We are forecasting the higher order moments. We also are not forecasting future return, because no evidence has shown that anyone can do that consistently.

Question: If your currency-risk management is not based on dynamic hedging, how does it work?

Layard-Liesching: A variety of different currency overlay styles exist. Dynamic hedging is a price-rebalancing strategy that has four different versions. We use a risk-rebalancing strategy that is not based on the Black–Scholes model.

Some of the disappointment has occurred because people have had two fundamental managers. This approach is wired to fail because fundamental managers believe currency has an equilibrium level. If the currency falls below a certain level, they buy it; if it is above, they sell. So, with two fundamental managers, the best that can happen is that they are both right, but three other outcomes are possible: One is right and one is wrong, one is wrong and one is right, or they are both wrong. To diversify on the return side, hire a fundamental manager and then perhaps someone with a technical modeling approach, because then the two managers access different information sources, which is a good way to diversify.

Currency overlay appointments are often for very large amounts of money. Our average client size is about half a billion U.S. dollars. So, check the manager's systems—check the resources, the performance-measurement systems, and make sure everyone and everything is backed up. Corporations should send in a team from their treasury department to check out the systems. Consultants also can be used to evaluate currency overlay managers and can give you thorough reports on them.

Question: How do you keep up to date on not only the underlying asset but the actual positioning in a country to keep the hedging amount accurate? In addition, how do you handle the cash management for the hedging gains and losses for a portfolio that is fully invested?

Layard-Liesching: The normal situation is to have only one or two currency overlay managers, depending on the size of the program, who adjust the hedges to the value of the underlying exposures. In that circumstance, the global custodian, if one is in place, will send the currency allocation to the overlay manager on a monthly basis. The overlay manager will then track the equity index, or whatever, in that particular country. At the end of every month, another auditor's statement will be delivered, which can be checked. If there is an interim allocation move—say, the equity manager gets out of Japan—the overlay manager has to be informed within the month. For the big funds, that process of extrapolation turns out to be very accurate indeed.

If a global custodian is not in place—for example, if the international investment is in a pooled fund—then the data are obtained from the pooled fund or, in some circumstances, directly from the fund manager. Because these are forward contracts, the overlay manager will generally inform the plan about the cash flow, whether it is going to the fund or from the fund, and give the fund estimates. Then, of course, the currency market has a three-day forward value settlement, so you know at least three days prior to the expiration of the forward agreement—and you thus can close it out earlier—exactly what the cash flows are. These amounts are normally run out of the short-term cash-management account, so it works very easily.

Integrating Global Asset Allocation and Currency Management

Bruno Solnik
Professor and Chair, Finance and Economics Department
HEC School of Management

Having up to a 10 percent currency allocation in a portfolio reduces the risk level of a global portfolio by diversifying domestic risks. Integrating global asset allocation and currency allocation decisions—joint optimization—produces the highest risk-adjusted returns and value added relative to other active and passive currency-management strategies. As currency risk premiums fluctuate over time, dynamic tactical asset allocations can also produce superior risk-adjusted returns.

An understanding of several empirical facts is necessary to integrate global asset allocation and currency management effectively. Differentiating between hedged and unhedged returns in the short run and long run, understanding how correlation affects portfolio risk and return, and analyzing currency's contribution to total portfolio risk are useful in confronting the problem of currency risk in portfolio management. Strategic currency allocation involves determining the appropriate currency allocation in the passive benchmark and determining the effective approach to currency management. In making those decisions, certain elements are helpful: knowing the characteristics of a good benchmark for assessing relative performance, understanding the differences between theory and reality when implementing hedging strategies, and analyzing the risk-adjusted returns of alternative hedging strategies. Tactical currency allocation is based on the observation that currency risk premiums and expected returns fluctuate over time; therefore, the optimal currency-hedging policy will also vary over time, providing opportunities for superior risk-adjusted returns with dynamic tactical strategies.

AN EMPIRICAL OVERVIEW

An investor in nondomestic markets can get two types of return. First is the return on a foreign investment translated into the investor's home currency. For example, if Swiss investors buy Italian stocks, they get the Swiss franc return on those stocks. The Italian lira return might look good, but it also entails Italian lira risk. The option is to hedge the currency risk, but the currency-hedged return differs from the local currency return by the interest rate differential between the two countries. Thus, the investor can get either the Swiss franc return or the currency-hedged return, and he or she must compare the two to evaluate the effect of the currency difference.

Figure 1 provides a historical comparison between the Swiss franc return, the hedged return, and the local currency return for nine countries. It indicates that the annualized Swiss franc return on Italian stocks during the past 25 years was about 1 percent; that is, an investment in the Italian stock index, taking into account dividends and capital appreciation and changed back into Swiss francs, would have produced an annualized return of about 1 percent. In Italian lira, the return was about 11 percent. Hedging the lira would have earned about 2 percent. The difference, of course, comes from the depreciation of the lira over time. The long-run difference between hedging and not hedging is about 1 percentage point, or 100 basis points. A comparison between the 1 percent and the 11 percent is not meaningful, because that difference does not include the 1–2 percentage point effect of currency on the return.

Figure 2 shows the same comparison for bonds as Figure 1 did for stocks. Here, too, the long-term impact of currency on returns is small. Over the long run, hedging or not hedging Italian bonds has made only about 100 basis points, or 1 percentage point, difference in returns.

Figure 1. Average Stock Return, 1971–96

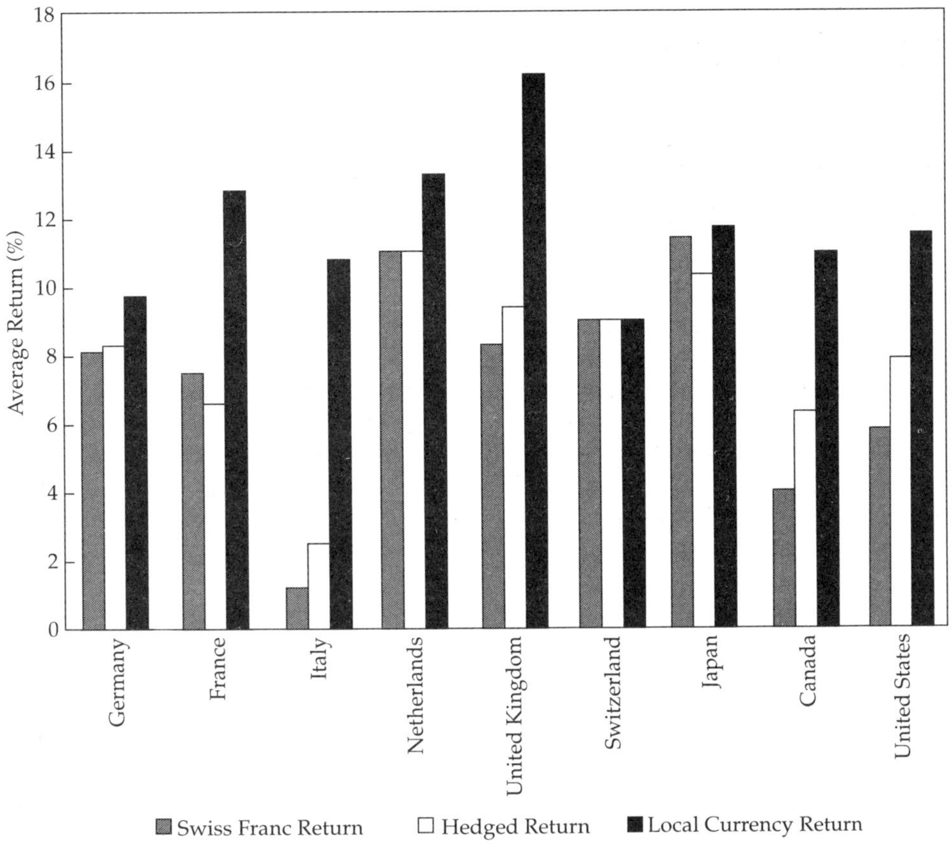

Figure 2. Average Bond Return, 1971–96

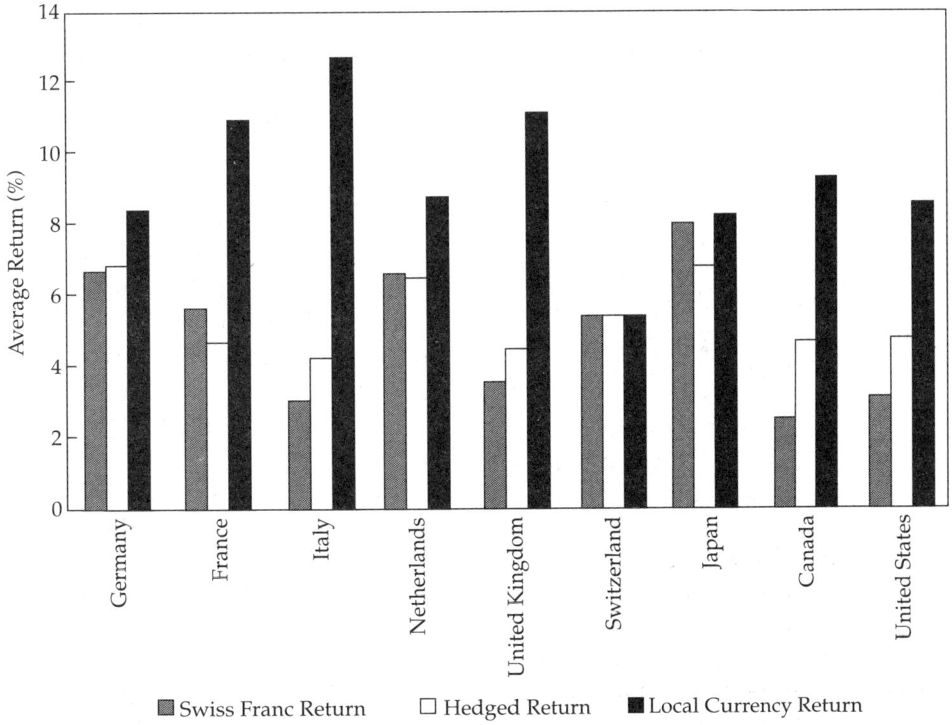

For most currencies, over the *very* long run, the interest rate differential corrects exchange rate movements. Maybe the most significant effect has been on the U.S. dollar. For other pairs of currencies, that phenomenon is less prominent. The interest rate on the U.S. dollar was low compared with movements in the U.S. dollar, so the cost of hedging in terms of interest rate differential has been low for foreign investors in U.S. markets, not only for stocks but also for bonds.

The short-term story is quite different. In the short run, currency makes a significant, but marginal, contribution to stock returns, and this contribution is further reduced if we look at a diversified portfolio rather than a single foreign market or currency. One way to measure the short-term impact of currency is to examine the standard deviation of market returns over, say, one month. **Figure 3** shows stock volatility measured in local currencies (currency hedged) and the volatility in Swiss francs. Those two numbers do not look very different. Volatility measured in Swiss francs is always higher than volatility in the local currency, but the increase for an individual stock market is not huge.

The story is quite different for bonds, as **Figure 4** shows. In the short run, currency makes a large contribution to bond returns because bond market risk is relatively smaller than equity market risk and because of the positive correlation between interest rate and currency movements. For example, the Swiss franc risk of Italian bonds is about twice the risk of currency-hedged Italian bonds—8 percent versus 14.3 percent. At least in the short term, currency has a significant impact on bond returns, although for equity returns, the impact is slight and, over the long run, becomes quite small.

The Importance of Correlation

Currency risk and local market risk are not additive. The variance in the Swiss franc is equal to the local market variance (e.g., in Italian lira) plus the foreign exchange variance plus 2 times the correlation of the two multiplied by the standard deviation of each source of risk: the local market risk of the Italian lira stock and the Swiss franc/Italian lira exchange rate risk. The following equation mathematically expresses the Swiss franc variance:

$$\sigma^2_{Swiss\ franc} = \sigma^2_{Local} + \sigma^2_{FX} + 2\rho_{(Local,\ FX)}\sigma_{Local}\sigma_{FX}.$$

Most people define the currency risk contribution simply as the difference between the total market risk, measured in local currency, and the local market risk, but the two are not additive. Assume that the

Figure 3. Stock Market Volatility, 1971–96

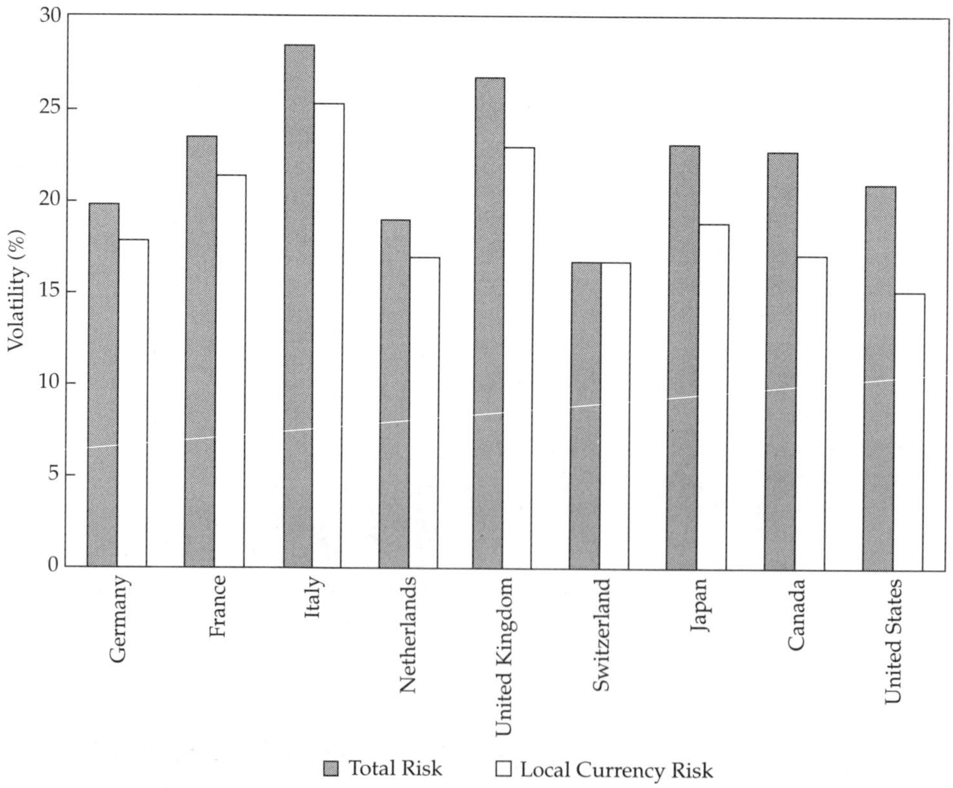

Figure 4. Bond Market Volatility, 1971–96

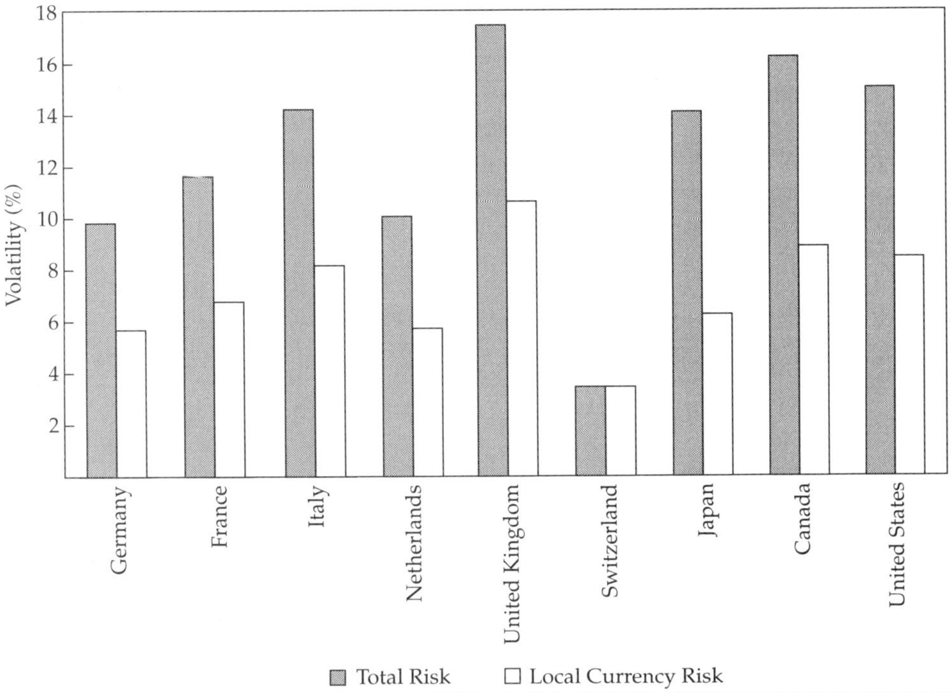

correlation between the local market variance and the exchange rate variance is equal to 1. Volatility in Swiss francs of Italian stocks would be equal to $(\sigma_{Market} + \sigma_{FX})$. This risk would be additive only if the correlation were equal to 1, but if the correlation were equal to –1, then no currency risk would exist. Instead, the correlation between currency risk and local market risk is usually quite small.

Consider the example of Nestlé S.A., a large multinational firm. If the Swiss franc suddenly goes down, we would expect Nestlé's revenues, which are derived from investments in and exports to the United States, Japan, and other countries, to increase when measured in Swiss francs. Because revenues measured in Swiss francs would go up, we would expect the stock price in Swiss francs to go up. Nestlé practices some currency hedging, but unless it is a perfect hedger, we would expect the correlation between the Swiss franc's value and the share price in Swiss francs to be negative. In the past, the correlation between stock prices and currency has been found to be small and negative (see Jorion 1994 and Solnik 1996).

For bonds, the tendency is to find positive correlation between currency and local market risk. When the Swiss franc depreciates, for example, whether because of the market or the government, the central bank in Switzerland intervenes. A good way to intervene is to strengthen interest rates to defend the Swiss franc, but rising interest rates are usually bad for bond prices. So, Swiss franc bond prices should go down, which would induce a positive correlation between the value of the Swiss franc and Swiss bond prices.

Five to seven years ago, when Switzerland experienced some inflation, interest rates in Switzerland went up to an unusual level—5 or 6 percent, which had never been seen there—and at the same time, the Swiss franc depreciated because of the inflation. Such positive correlation is bad news for a foreign investor buying Swiss bonds, because he or she basically has cumulative currency risk—not only translation risk but also the value of the asset itself goes down if the currency goes down.

This correlation is bad news for both non-Swiss investors in Switzerland and purely domestic Swiss investors. Consider a domestic investor who only invests in Swiss bonds. Basically, the investor is taking currency risk by buying Swiss bonds. If the Swiss franc goes down against the dollar, the value of the investment will go down. The same phenomenon exists somewhat in Canada. For example, by buying Canadian bonds, Canadian investors are basically taking some currency risk—the U.S./Canadian dollar risk. So, when talking about currency risk, we should extend the definition and look not only at foreign-currency-denominated assets but also at the impact of local currency movement on the value of the domestic assets.

Summary of Currency Risk

Four empirical facts summarize currency risk considerations:

- With hedging, in the long run, the interest rate differential between countries makes a difference.
- With currency volatility, the total market risk is less than local risk because of the low correlation between the two.
- Currencies exhibit some form of mean reversion, explaining why currency risk is lower in the long run than in the short run. The big problem is that the long run, in this case, is extremely long for a portfolio manager, even for a pension fund.
- Look at the contribution of currency risk to the total portfolio. Many investors focus only on a foreign asset's risk, but they should care about its contribution to the overall portfolio's risk.

Twenty years ago, we moved from an individual asset perspective to a total portfolio perspective, especially in the United States with the ERISA regulations, but we still do not often apply the total portfolio approach to currency. Currencies get partly diversified in a portfolio or basket of currencies, but the portfolio still ends up with some currency risk. Basically, the risk for Swiss investors is that the Swiss franc will be very strong in the future. This risk is undiversifiable for a Swiss investor, because if the Swiss franc is strong, then Japanese stocks will look unattractive as the yen goes down against the Swiss franc; U.S. stocks will look unattractive because the U.S. dollar goes down against the Swiss franc. So, the strength of the home currency poses risk for investors.

STRATEGIC CURRENCY ALLOCATION

Strategic currency allocation involves two important decisions:

- What is the appropriate currency allocation in the passive benchmark to use to measure performance and to guide investment in the long term?
- What approach should be taken to structure currency-management efforts—an integrated approach or, at the other extreme, a separate currency-overlay manager?

Determining a Passive Benchmark

Before deciding on the appropriate currency allocation in a passive benchmark, one must know the qualities of a good benchmark. A good benchmark must be *widely accepted*. Big companies like Shell Pensionfunds Beheer B.V. can afford to have their own benchmarks because they do not need to compare their performance with that of others, but most smaller investors cannot afford to construct their own benchmarks. They are compared with others, so they need to have some commonality with other benchmarks and hence must use accepted benchmarks. A benchmark also needs to be a feasible one that can be *easily replicated* by passive strategies.

Finally, the benchmark needs to be *consistent with equilibrium*. The benchmark must be feasible if everyone were using the same strategy; the market must absorb it. When Sharpe and others devised the capital asset pricing model, they came up with the important conclusion that everyone should be holding the market portfolio. Some stories about alphas and betas were created, but the big conclusion was that everyone, regardless of their degree of risk aversion, whether poor or rich, would hold the market portfolio, which is consistent with equilibrium. If everyone follows that strategy, that is fine. Big pension funds in the United States hold the market portfolio, and the market absorbs it very well.

Lessons from Research

The basic conclusion from theoretical research is that the optimal portfolio is the world market portfolio partially hedged against currency risk. We can observe the world market portfolio; we can use world market capitalization. Although one may disagree as to which broad index to use—the Financial Times/ Standard & Poor's Actuaries World Index, the Salomon Brothers World Index, or the MSCI World Index—all of these portfolios approximate the investable world portfolio and are observable. The problem is identifying the optimal hedge ratio, for optimal hedge ratios are a function of the asset in terms of utility and net wealth.

Financial research has also focused attention on currency risk premiums. Exchange rates, like interest rates and stock prices, are financial prices, and risk premiums are justified. The forward premium should be equal to the expected return on the currency plus a risk premium. In other words, the forward premium should be different from the expected currency movement.

The supply and demand for currency affect exchange rates and the size of the currency risk premium. Thus, currency prices adjust because of supply and demand factors—influencing the currency risk premium—until the new equilibrium exchange rate is determined.

Suppose the Swiss are big net investors in Papualand and the Papualanders invest little abroad. The Swiss are worried about currency risk and have a strong demand for hedging Papuan dollars into Swiss francs. The Papualanders have little demand for hedging Swiss francs, because they are not net foreign investors in Switzerland. The Swiss borrow Papuan dollars in order to have a long position in Papualand stocks. The Swiss can sell their exposure to the Papuan dollar by borrowing Papuan dollars and investing these dollars in Swiss franc deposits. So, they pay the Papuan dollar interest rate and receive the Swiss franc interest rate. But because the supply of Papuan dollars is limited, the Papuan dollar interest rate increases and the Swiss franc interest rate declines. This development creates an interest rate differential that is basically a risk premium that the Swiss are willing to pay to hedge their currency risk and to induce Papualanders to provide the vehicle for that hedge.

Pragmatic Shortcuts

In reality, we cannot observe the optimal hedge ratio, so pragmatic shortcuts are necessary. One possibility is full hedging. Although we cannot tell whether the risk premium in the Swiss franc is positive or negative, we want to minimize the risk, so we hedge 100 percent (see Perold and Schulman 1988). Therefore, we would use a fully hedged or unit-hedge benchmark as the average benchmark. Froot (1993) argued that over the long run, currency risk washes out. This finding is difficult to replicate, because it requires a very long - run period—about 150 years—to show this result. Other people use universal hedge ratios (what I call arbitrary hedge ratios); Black (1990) came up with a 0.75 hedge ratio, and Gastineau (1995) estimated a 0.50 hedge ratio.

Full hedging is simply focusing on minimizing the volatility of the foreign part of the portfolio. Many people argue against this approach. First, having a bit of foreign currency improves the portfolio's total risk. Adding 5 percent in foreign currency to a portfolio reduces the risk level of the portfolio by diversifying the domestic risks. Jorion (1989) found that a foreign currency allocation up to about 10 percent reduces portfolio risk. Full hedging assumes that the investor is looking only at the foreign component and becomes very meaningful if 70 percent of investments are allocated abroad.

If we were doing a passive, naive, risk-minimization hedge and only cared about risk, not about expected return, we would take into account the correlation between the currency risk and the asset risk. In a reasonable time span, currency risk is present. To derive his 0.75 hedge ratio, Black had to make many heroic assumptions. For example, the Papualanders and the Swiss would have to have exactly the same amount of investment abroad. Also, you would have to postulate identical risk aversion in the world market and so on.

I prefer Gastineau's "Why Bother?" approach. If I have to make so many assumptions in order to derive the hedge ratio I want—0.75—I can assume that 0.50 is the best. Why 0.50? Because it is halfway between 0 and 1, neither of which is appropriate. No theory (and by theory I mean some commonsense equilibrium approach in which simple hedge ratios would be universal) will ever be identical for every investor and every asset. Because hedge ratios differ across assets and currencies, depending on unobservable foreign asset positions, utility functions, individual risk aversion, and inflation, no simple practical solution exists and no one can provide a commonsense benchmark for hedging.

Integrated Management versus Currency Overlay

Currencies should not be treated as an entirely special entity. Any good financial analyst must have some vision about the exchange rate because it is a major consideration in valuing a corporation. All the monetary variables are important components of valuing a stock or a bond market. Currencies are one of several important variables that must all be taken into account in valuing stocks and bonds. Jorion (1994) analyzed the effects of separating the investment and the currency decisions, showing that conducting a separate asset allocation optimization for assets and for currencies is clearly suboptimal. He introduced what we call *joint optimization*, in which the asset allocation and the currency allocation are optimized together: We buy Swiss stocks and we partly hedge all of them together. In *partial optimization*, we first determine the optimal asset allocation among Swiss stocks, French stocks, and Japanese stocks and then decide the optimal currency hedge based on the asset allocation; thus, one manager does the asset allocation and gives it to the currency overlay manager, who then optimizes, given that asset allocation. In *separate optimization*, the asset allocation and currency management decisions are totally separate. Neither manager knows what the other is doing. Jorion looked at the period from 1978 to 1991 and derived simple efficient frontiers for three different strategies, as shown in **Figure 5**. The joint optimization approach produces superior results—higher returns for a given level of risk—relative to the less cooperative methods.

Table 1 presents Jorion's optimal positions with stocks and currencies from a U.S. dollar perspective over the 1978–91 period. He first optimized without currency, examining the optimal asset allocation without hedging for a portfolio with only five markets, a return of 11.1 percent, a standard deviation of 16.1, and a Sharpe ratio of about 0.7.

The joint optimization portfolio is heavy in Japanese stocks because the yen risk can be hedged. The 1978–91 period was not a good time to be in yen. This strategy favors all foreign investments because the

Figure 5. International Bond Portfolios: Efficient Frontiers Using Different Optimization Methods, 1978–91

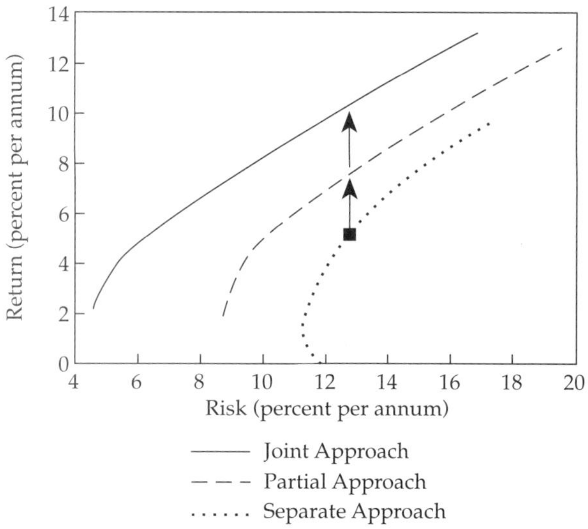

Source: Jorion (1994).

currency risk can be removed if it is optimal to do so. This portfolio provides the highest Sharpe ratio (excess return over standard deviation) —0.81.

If the currency decision is delegated to the overlay manager, as with the partial optimization approach, the overlay manager starts with the asset allocation given and then decides on the optimal currency hedging, producing suboptimal overall results and lower risk-adjusted returns—a 0.78 Sharpe ratio—relative to the joint optimization method.

Note that the joint optimization portfolio also produces the highest value added—the extra return for a given risk level—of 173 basis points relative to no currency hedging. Although the improvement in risk-adjusted returns is not gigantic, the optimizing process searches for every basis point of incremental return. This method suffers from all the biases of mean–variance optimization, but even so, the joint optimization method produces higher risk-adjusted returns than the other methods. Given the fact that the correlation between currency and equity is weak, delegating the currency management is not so bad.

Table 2 presents optimal portfolio positions with bonds and currencies over the same time period. In the case of bonds, the effect of joint optimization on risk-adjusted returns is huge. Although the difference in Sharpe ratios between no currency hedging (0.33) and the joint optimization portfolio (0.60) is 0.27, the value added at a 10 percent risk level by using the joint optimization approach is 273 basis points higher than without the currency hedging. For bonds, when the correlation between currency and assets is positive, delegating the currency overlay is suboptimal, but in practice, such delegation is seldom done.

To summarize, in the presence of correlation, partial optimization is suboptimal, but it is acceptable in the absence of correlation. Full hedging would be acceptable only without correlation between the asset and the currency and without a currency-risk premium.

TACTICAL CURRENCY ALLOCATION

The currency market is an efficient market with somewhat predictable risk premiums and expected returns. The efficient market hypothesis never states that expected returns should be constant over time.

Table 1. Optimal Positions with Stocks and Currencies, 1978–91

	Without Currency	With Currency Joint	With Currency Partial	With Currency Separate
Return	11.1%	12.9%	11.8%	12.2%
Risk	16.1%	16.1%	15.1%	16.6%
Sharpe ratio	0.689	0.805	0.781	0.735
Value added (at 15% risk)	—	1.73%	1.38%	0.72%
Positions				
Stocks				
United States	29%[a]	3%[a]	29%	29%
Japan	29[a]	39[a]	29	29
Germany	0[a]	4[a]	0	0
United Kingdom	16[a]	18[a]	16	16
France	26[a]	36[a]	26	26
Currency				
Yen	—	–39[a]	–29[a]	0[a]
German mark	—	–58[a]	–42[a]	–42[a]
British pound	—	30[a]	28[a]	8[a]
French franc	—	15[a]	13[a]	40[a]
Net foreign exchange exposure	71%	45%	41%	77%

[a]Optimized position.

Source: Jorion (1994).

Table 2. Optimal Positions with Bonds and Currencies, 1978–91

	Without Currency	With Currency		
		Joint	Partial	Separate
Return	3.7%	3.6%	3.6%	4.2%
Risk	11.3%	5.9%	8.2%	11.7%
Sharpe ratio	0.331	0.604	0.432	0.366
Value added (at 10% risk)	—	2.73%	1.02%	0.37%
Positions				
Bonds				
United States	44%[a]	0%[a]	44%	44%
Japan	39[a]	48[a]	39	39
Germany	0[a]	0[a]	0	0
United Kingdom	17[a]	3[a]	17	17
France	0[a]	49[a]	0	0
Currency				
Yen	—	–48[a]	–39[a]	0[a]
German mark	—	–52[a]	–17[a]	–17[a]
British pound	—	18[a]	12[a]	7[a]
French franc	—	–9[a]	7[a]	16[a]
Net foreign exchange exposure	56%	9%	19%	62%

[a]Optimized position.

Source: Jorion (1994).

Expected returns fluctuate because of such factors as business cycles, changes in the market environment, and individuals' relative degrees of risk aversion. So, the risk premium can fluctuate over time. Furthermore, central banks are important players in the currency markets, and empirical evidence indicates that they are consistent losers because their objective function is to stabilize the market. The French central bank wants to win against the German central bank, so the biggest concern is what the French franc/German mark exchange rate does. The central banks consistently lose, however, because they have predictable domestic objectives that do not follow traditional investment paradigms.

The stock market, interest rates, and currencies are very difficult to predict, but because currencies are visible, being wrong in currencies is more painful than being wrong in the market or interest rates. Everyone has an opinion on currencies, and the predictions will be wrong 50 percent of the time (or 45 percent at best), so people just quit trying to forecast exchange rates, which might be a mistake.

Academic research provides some evidence of predictability in foreign exchange rates. **Figure 6** shows the percentage of variance explained by a very simple model that I use for tactical asset allocation (TAA) that takes into account interest rate levels, term spreads, interest rate differentials, and other variables as predictors of future stock price movements, bond price movements, and currency movements. This model can be adapted to changes in the business cycle, and results indicate that it has some predictive ability for stocks, bonds, and currency returns. The predictive power for currencies is as good as for bonds, which is not so surprising. Basically, the adjusted R^2 is on the order of 5–7 percent, which is weak but statistically significant.

The optimal currency-hedging policy will vary considerably over time because the sign and magnitude of the risk premium on each currency (which depends on the demand for currency hedging) are likely to change over time. The demand for currency hedging is affected by the net foreign investment position of each currency, the relative risk aversion of nationals of different countries, and the economic conditions in the various countries.

The performance of three simulated dynamic tactical strategies is shown in **Table 3**. These results, which use out-of-sample performance, separate the universe of possible investments into equity-only and bond-only investments, and the strategies have the same volatility as the U.S. index; that is, domestic equity performance and global equity performance are compared for the same risk level in U.S. dollars. The first strategy allows only fully hedged investments. The second strategy allows only unhedged investments. Thus, one can invest across the world, but one cannot hedge the currency risk; the currency and market choices are necessarily linked. The third strategy allows separation of the market and currency decisions and partial currency hedging is allowed.

Because of the predictability of the currency risk premium, the global stock-only performance of the unhedged strategy, 0.962 percent monthly return, is superior to both the U.S. stock market return of 0.247 percent and the fully hedged strategy return of 0.694 percent. Allowing a separation of market selection and currency selection—the optimal hedging strategy—further improves performance, to 1.149 per-

Figure 6. Explanatory Power of TAA Model for Various Markets

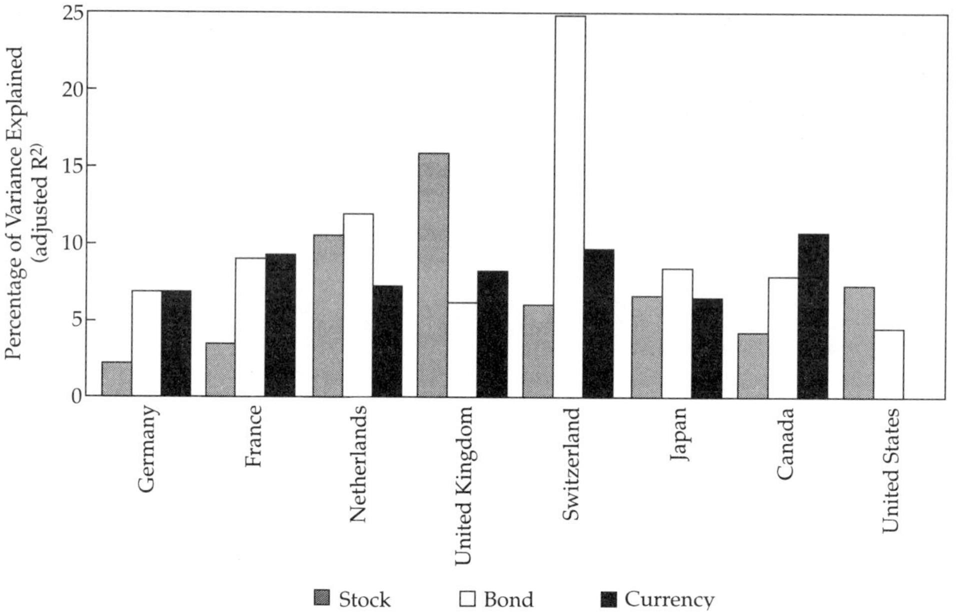

cent. The results are similar for the global bond strategies. The optimal hedging strategy return, 0.663 percent monthly, outperforms the U.S. bond index return of –0.017 percent, the fully hedged strategy return of 0.395 percent, and the no-hedging return of 0.508 percent, all with the same level of risk. Thus, dynamic TAA can improve the performance of these strategies in a risk-controlled way.

Although the asset allocation and currency allocation strategies are basically quite good, the problem is that an R^2 of 5–7 percent requires many years to confirm the effectiveness of these strategies, making performance evaluation extremely difficult. These strategies might significantly underperform passive strategies for 2 years but end up big winners 20 years from now. Although people do not expect these TAA strategies to be right every month or every quarter, they do expect them to be right most quarters and most years. But that cannot be true with optimization models, which are intended for long-term, not short-term, use. Table 3 summarizes the results of my model, which is a good forecasting model for the short term.

CONCLUSION

Foreign investors must be aware that local currency returns may look attractive but are unavailable to foreign investors and that currency-hedged returns differ from local-currency returns by the interest rate differential between two countries. Although currency makes a significant but marginal contribution to stock returns in the short run, it makes a large contribution to bond returns because bond market risk is relatively smaller than that of stocks and because the correlation between interest rates and currency movements is positive. Over the very long run, however, the interest rate differential corrects exchange rate movements, because currencies exhibit mean reversion. Although the long run is meaningful, it may not be practical, given the time horizon of portfolio managers. Just as ERISA has moved from the individual asset perspective to the total portfolio approach, investors should have a total portfolio approach to currency, examining currency's contribution to total portfolio risk.

Before deciding on a strategic currency allocation, a passive benchmark—one that is widely accepted, easily replicated, and consistent with equi-

Table 3. Realized Returns in Excess of U.S. Risk-Free Rate for Given Risk Levels (percent per month)

		Mean Monthly Excess Returns			
Asset	Volatility (standard deviation)	U.S. Market	Full Hedge	No Hedge	Optimal Hedge
Stocks	4.67%	0.247%	0.694%	0.962%	1.149%
Bonds	2.56	–0.017	0.395	0.508	0.663

Source: Solnik (1993c).

librium—is necessary to compare relative performance of alternative hedging strategies. A comparison of performance using alternative hedging methods indicates that joint optimization produces the highest risk-adjusted returns and value added—extra return for a *given* risk level—for both stocks and bonds relative to a systematic no-hedging policy.

As the sign and magnitude of the currency risk premium change, the optimal currency-hedging policy will vary considerably over time, providing opportunities to enhance returns using dynamic tactical asset allocation strategies. Although dynamic TAA strategies can provide superior risk-adjusted returns, their effectiveness takes a long time to assess.

Question and Answer Session

Bruno Solnik

Question: If currency returns are nonstationary and mean–variance results are unstable, why use mean–variance analysis if it gives contradictory results?

Solnik: We are still at the stage of trying to understand currency returns. We try to derive some concepts and some practical rules in the face of a very complex world. I was using mean–variance optimization as a very simple tool to compare risk and return, although we know that relationship is much more complex. I was not advocating using mean–variance optimization for the future in trying to build portfolios. It has too many biases and problems, so I certainly would not use it to build an optimal currency portfolio.

I have heard about some alternatives, such as shortfall analysis, that use the same mechanics as mean–variance optimization. The idea is to reject standard deviation because it is too simple. Standard deviation is based on a symmetrical distribution, so we have as much risk of losing as of winning. Because it is symmetrical, we can talk about standard deviation as a risk of losing. If it is not symmetrical, we need to use another indicator of distribution, and then maybe we could estimate the probability of a loss or use shortfall analysis. Shortfall analysis would be exactly identical to standard deviation if the distribution of returns is symmetrical and different if it is not symmetrical. Therefore, shortfall analysis is more complete than the standard deviation approach; it is an improvement. The big problem is not the shape of the distribution, however, but its instability, so using any measure that relies on the past for building a future portfolio is uncertain.

Question: Are the correlations between stocks and currencies changing and, if so, how quickly?

Solnik: In a recent article (Solnik 1996), I showed that the correlation between stock markets has been remarkably stable, but with cycles. Correlation increases in periods of high volatility and then reverses to the normal trend. For currencies, I do not know. I am extremely surprised at the low correlation between stocks and currencies. I do not buy the explanation that this low correlation is because corporations do internal hedging within their corporate structures. This presumption is probably not true for every corporation or even for most corporations. The tax code does not facilitate it. So, I would expect the correlation between stocks and currencies to change, but I do not know how quickly. The problem with institutional investors and, therefore, bankers is that as soon as one of them catches the flu, they all catch the flu—that is, they all do the same thing. Because they all mimic what the others are doing, the correlation between stocks and currencies might increase quickly. If people change their investment perceptions and investment styles, the correlation can go up extremely rapidly.

Performance Attribution Analysis

John C. Stannard, CFA
Director, Russell Data Services
Frank Russell Company

Performance attribution analyzes a portfolio manager's success (particularly regarding outperformance of the portfolio benchmark) in the context of the investment decision-making process. It is an acid test for portfolio managers and a valuable business management tool, highlighting strengths and weaknesses in the investment process and identifying continued evidence of skill. Performance attribution decomposes excess portfolio returns into three components: the asset allocation effect, security selection effect, and currency effect. The currency effect can be further decomposed into the forward premium effect and the currency management effect. Regardless of the algorithms used, the most important goal in a performance attribution analysis is to present the results in a form that is consistent with the decision-making process.

Performance attribution compares historical returns with a benchmark, evaluates how well the portfolio manager has done relative to that benchmark, and attributes the manager's success—or lack thereof—to particular decisions in the investment management process. The performance attribution method, also known as "accounting decomposition," is perhaps the most commonly used attribution method, and its name arises from the fact that results are based on historical performance numbers derived from basic investment accounting data. An essentially backward-looking tool, this approach is not the same as *ex ante* return forecasting (which sometimes carries the same name), but it is a useful and beneficial process that uses historical returns to evaluate the success of investment decisions.

Although one can argue about the pros and cons of different performance measurement methods, the algorithms are, in principle, quite similar for all methods. Applying the correct framework (i.e., producing attribution results that are consistent with the decision process) is more important than which algorithm is used. Of course, it would be naive to suggest that the algorithms themselves are not important, but significantly more information error occurs by applying an incorrect analytical framework than by using the wrong set of algorithms. Most organizations that apply these techniques should reach somewhat similar conclusions about the effectiveness of the investment process regardless of whether a particular effect may be a basis point or two different between one method and another.

This presentation focuses on the basic framework of performance attribution, provides single-currency and multicurrency examples of how the theory is applied in practice, and evaluates the basic rules of attribution. We identify the framework operating within a specific business situation and then apply performance attribution analysis.

THE BASICS

The best starting point for performance attribution is at the big-picture level. Where did the portfolio manager add value? Is there evidence of consistent success? Where should management focus its attention?

Performance attribution is a method of determining how much value the investment decision-making process added to a portfolio. It begins with the basic portfolio-management decision model illustrated in **Figure 1**. This model relates the strategic plan (determining investment policy and the asset mix) to investment management (weighting a fund toward better-performing asset classes and selecting securities that outperform the index). Although equity and bond fund managers make decisions about their portfolios in a variety of ways, their approaches share elements of this basic decision model.

Performance attribution can be calculated on a daily basis and stock prices can be analyzed on an

Figure 1. Basic Decision Model

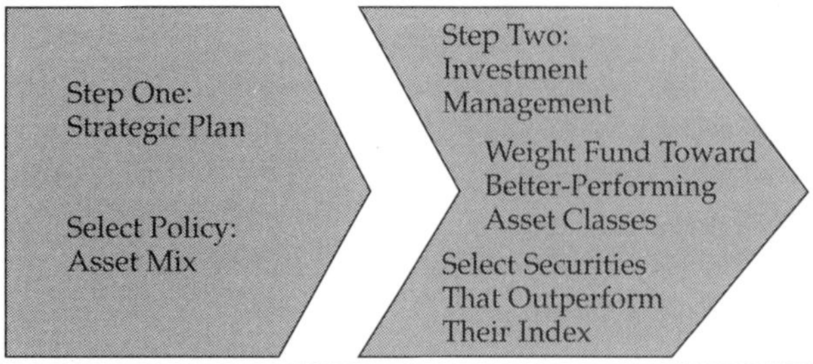

intraday basis, but collecting and analyzing the volume and types of data needed is a challenging and exhaustive task. The daily data-collection problem becomes formidable when dealing with multiple currencies, tracking cross-currency exchange rates, and comparing forward premiums from market to market.

Different time horizons for performance evaluation have their pros and cons, but most firms focus first on the big picture to get a broad sense of how successfully asset classes have performed. This approach requires more-limited data yet provides a good explanation of where success occurred. Frank Russell Company uses the big-picture approach with large corporate pension funds and money managers. We determine which market segments added value to a portfolio during a certain period, and then we analyze which specific decisions had the biggest impact on the results. Consistent success over time may indicate that the investment process requires skill, but sustained underperformance, particularly arising in a specific aspect of the process, may suggest a problem that requires management's attention.

SINGLE-CURRENCY FRAMEWORK

A single-currency framework divides a portfolio into a number of different segments and decomposes sources of return into the index contribution, the asset allocation effect, and the security selection effect. Typically, the segments in a domestic equity portfolio might be industry groups.

In a single-currency framework, the first step in attribution, as **Figure 2** shows, is to identify the asset allocation effect. To do this, we need to know which asset classes in the portfolio are the winners, which are the losers, and further, whether we have positioned our portfolio to exploit the winners. With this approach, we first examine how we have done in particular markets relative to the policy benchmark return, measuring the benefit of overweighting or underweighting certain asset classes. This notion of benchmark-relative analysis is very important. Older techniques will measure attribution effects as a function of the actual return achieved in a market—e.g., giving a positive allocation effect in industrials if industrials had a positive return. But the key question is the opportunity cost or benefit of not investing at the benchmark weight, and benchmark-relative attribution captures this amount precisely.

Figure 2. Asset Allocation Effect

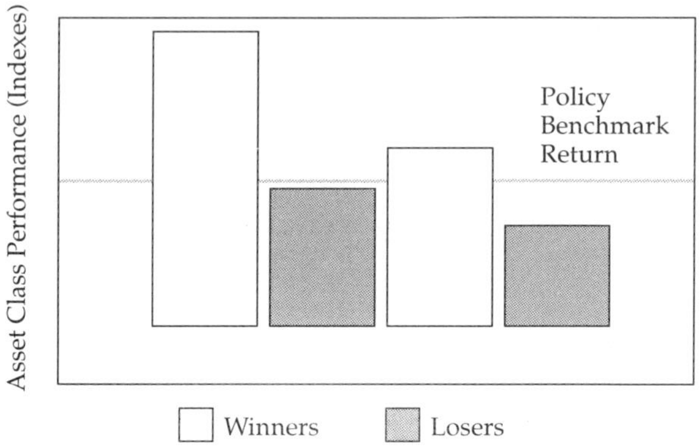

Performance attribution decomposes return into the asset allocation effect and the security selection effect, as shown in **Figure 3**. The index contribution is the return in a given market for the benchmark weighting of that market. Of course, in one of the winning asset segments, this contribution will be positive (as in the diagram), but across the whole index, the index contribution is zero. If we overweight a particular market (shown as the difference between W_p and W_b) and that market performs well, the net effect at the total portfolio level (the asset allocation contribution) is a function of the excess weight ($W_p - W_b$) and the extent to which the portfolio has outperformed ($R_p - R_b$). Note that, as mentioned earlier, when we make a decision about an asset category, we do not evaluate that decision in nominal terms—that is, not by whether its return is positive or negative but by how well it did relative to the passive benchmark return. Outperforming the index

Figure 3. Single-Currency Attribution

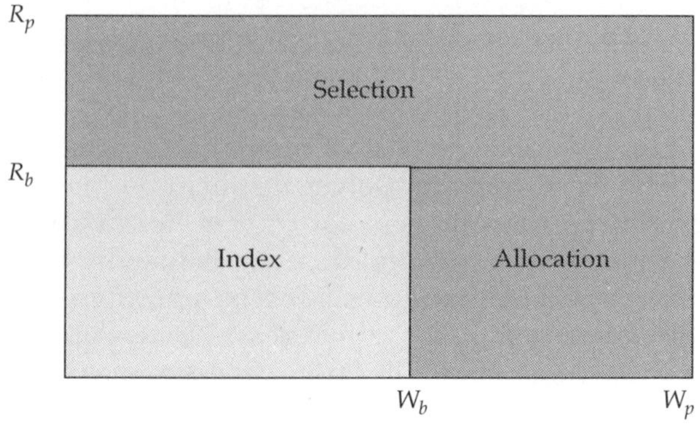

of any particular sector gives us the security selection effect. This amount is a function of both the excess return over the benchmark ($R_p - R_b$) and the portfolio weight, W_b.

Overweighting a particular asset class can, in some cases, have a large effect on total return. **Table 1** provides a simple example of a portfolio that is overweight in stocks and underweight in cash. Not surprisingly, stocks significantly outperform cash, so because the portfolio is overweight in stocks by 11 percent, the attribution analysis measures an asset allocation effect of 67 basis points. Further, the stock portfolio has outperformed the index by 1.3 percent, which results in a security selection effect of 93 basis points. Similar results arise in the cash segment of the portfolio. Of course, for a 20- to 25-asset portfolio, the answers using this framework are much less intuitive than for a simple portfolio, so the attribution analysis provides valuable insight into the sources of outperformance.

MULTICURRENCY FRAMEWORK

Attribution gets more complicated for multiple currencies. Different ways of gaining currency exposure affect performance attribution, giving rise to different explanations of returns. Multicurrency attribution must take into account the results of both physical exposures in nonbase currency markets and currency hedging via forward currency contracts. To capture the complexities of the currency markets, the traditional currency effect measure is further disaggregated into the forward premium effect (reflecting the effects of relative interest rates and currency premiums) and the currency management effect (which takes into account the management of currency movements over and above those explained by forward premiums).

A global equity portfolio that is overweighted (or underweighted) in a non-base-currency market gives rise to an "implicit" currency bet. But currency positions (or "explicit" currency bets) often exist over and above those arising as a result of asset positions. The effects of the implicit currency bet plus additional currency decisions, usually through the use of forward currency contracts, are additive, so both need to be measured.

When measuring the effect of currency exchange rate changes, we must distinguish between those that are expected and those that are not. In particular, expected exchange rate changes, accounted for by differential interest rates, cannot be hedged away, because the pricing of forward currency contracts assumes that such expected currency changes will happen. This relative interest rate is measured in the forward premium effect.

The Forward Premium Effect

In attribution, the forward premium effect is the consequence of interest rate differentials between countries (based on "expected" currency returns) and of the portfolio being over- or underweight in a particular market. Of course, the countries in a benchmark will have different levels of interest rates, which will give rise to a range of forward premiums relative to the base currency. The relevant question is whether the portfolio is over- or underweight in the high-forward-premium currencies. To the extent that the currency effects that arise from this over- or underweighting cannot be eliminated, the nominal returns in a high-interest-rate market, all things being equal, will generally tend to be slightly higher than in other markets. Because of this difference, the forward premium effect is often regarded as a form of allocation effect.

Karnosky and Singer (1994) approached performance attribution from a different angle, viewing market returns in terms of risk premiums. Although their approach looks different, the two methods are in fact quite similar. In effect, they include the forward premium effect as part of the allocation effect. Understanding the forward premium effect is important, because it can have a substantial impact for periods longer than a year. The impact for short periods is small, however.

The Currency-Management Effect

The management of currency movements in excess of those "predicted" by forward premiums (including currency hedging) is measured in the currency-management effect. To understand this effect, consider a U.K. investor investing in the United States. Assume that the movement in the dollar is 5

Table 1. Returns on a Single-Currency Example Portfolio

	Portfolio		Benchmark		Attribution Effects		
Asset	Weight	Return	Weight	Return	Allocation	Selection	Total
Stock	71.40%	16.50%	60.00%	15.20%	0.67%	0.93%	1.60%
Cash	28.60	1.86	40.00	0.50	1.01	0.38	1.39
Total	100.0%	12.31	100.0%	9.32	1.68%	1.31%	2.99%

percent positive and also assume that 50 basis points of the 5 percent was anticipated by differences in interest rates—that is, interest rates in the United States are lower than interest rates in the United Kingdom. This relationship, and the impact of forward premiums, means that this investor can hedge away only 4.5 percent out of the total 5 percent currency appreciation. Of course, dollar appreciation would be fine, but depreciation would be a concern, and it is the overall uncertainty of currency changes that an investor is seeking to avoid when placing a currency hedge. Of course, if the investor decides to bring the portfolio back to neutral—for example, by hedging an overweight position—the currency-management effect will be zero.

Consider the three-asset U.S. dollar-denominated portfolio described in **Table 2**, which has a 70 percent weight in Germany, a 20 percent weight in Japan, and a 10 percent weight in cash. The benchmark is 50/50 in Germany and Japan. The figures in Table 2 give us a guide to the likely attribution results, which are shown in **Table 3**. Compared with the –3 percent average currency return of the benchmark, the German mark has been quite strong. So, given the overweight position in Germany, the performance impact of currency should be positive. The Germany weighting had a less positive influence in local market terms, however. The German mark return on the portfolio was about 7 percent (slightly less than the benchmark return of 7.25 percent), so the selection effect was negative. Further, because the 7 percent German equity return was well below the benchmark average (of slightly more than 9 percent), the allocation effect in Germany was negative too. Results in Japan were a little better, showing positive security selection: The yen return was about 11 percent, above the benchmark return of 9.9 percent.

Table 3 confirms that the currency contribution in aggregate was beneficial to the portfolio, but the security selection effect was mixed—good in Japan, not so good in Germany. Allocation effects were negative for the portfolio as a whole.

Breaking out the two currency effects, as shown in Table 3, reveals more detail about the currency impacts. We can see from the results that the portfolio is overweight in Germany with a positive forward premium and underweight in Japan with a negative forward premium (in this example at least). In total, the portfolio gained about 2.3 percent from currency, which more than offsets the 1.5 percent loss in allocation. The security selection effect of including Japan, about 22 basis points, slightly outweighed the negative selection effect in Germany. Reviewing such performance attribution results over a period of time gives portfolio managers a sense of where they add value and whether the investment process is working.

BENCHMARKS

The importance of the benchmark in the attribution-measurement process is often underrated. Many managers postpone the choice of a benchmark until they remember they will need one and look around for the best one available or one that everybody else uses. The benchmark is extremely important, however, to both the client and the managers. It defines the natural position of the strategy and should be carefully chosen. Moreover, anyone who is going to use a global benchmark needs to understand the emphases of the various possible benchmarks and how their construction methodology will affect their effectiveness as benchmarks.

Benchmarks in Theory

An effective benchmark might be defined as an independent hurdle rate that provides an objective test of the effective implementation of an investment strategy. In other words, the benchmark sets a hurdle; meeting the benchmark performance means achieving that hurdle. If the hurdle is achieved, the strategy has been successful.

Table 2. Returns on a Multicurrency Portfolio

Asset	Country Weights: Portfolio	Country Weights: Benchmark	Currency Return	Local Currency Returns: Portfolio	Local Currency Returns: Benchmark
Germany	70%	50%	1.0%	7.04%	7.25%
Japan	20	50	–7.0	11.07	9.97
Cash	10	0	0	0.5	0.4

Table 3. Attribution Effects in a Multicurrency Portfolio

Asset	Allocation	Selection	Forward Premium	Currency Management	Total
Germany	–0.27%	–0.15%	0.08%	0.72%	0.38%
Japan	–0.41	0.22	0.12	1.08	1.01
Cash	–0.82	0.01	0.01	0.29	–0.51
Total	–1.50%	0.08%	0.21%	2.09%	0.88%

Note that the benchmark measures an "investment strategy." A fund manager must have a logically constructed strategy and must understand that strategy. A good benchmark must be relevant to the manager's strategy and to the markets in which it is applied.

The hurdle concept provides an "objective test" of whether the strategy has been successful. In a hurdle race, a runner can win the race despite knocking down a couple of hurdles, but the chance of winning is small if the runner knocks them all down. Investment managers hope to jump over all the hurdles but realize they will sometimes miss, and they know they cannot always miss and still win.

To be a good objective measure, a benchmark must be clear, simple to all who are using it, and unambiguous. If two people can arrive at different interpretations from the same benchmark, problems are bound to arise. Also, applying two different (and conflicting) benchmarks drives managers toward compromise. If they have to compromise, the chances are that, over time, they will underperform the most difficult of the two benchmarks.

A comparison of equity indexes for European markets, presented in **Table 4**, illustrates how benchmarks focusing on the same market can be structured in different ways. For example, the Morgan Stanley Capital International (MSCI) Index has fewer stocks than the other two indexes. Although Salomon's Broad Market Index (BMI) has about three times the number of stocks as the MSCI Index, the MSCI has a longer history, which is one reason that it is widely used by U.S. portfolio managers. The MSCI and the Financial Times/Standard & Poor's Actuaries World Index (FT/S&P-AWI) use capitalization weighting and a sampling approach. BMI adjusts for free float, the investible proportion of the market, including companies with free float exceeding $100 million.

The free float in several European markets is shown in **Figure 4**. Germany and France, for example, have free float of less than 70 percent. The amount of float can have a major impact on an index's country distribution and, therefore, on the suitable choice of an index for a portfolio strategy. Most stocks are freely available in the United Kingdom; some government holdings and cross-ownerships exist there, but not many. Cross-ownerships in Germany, though, are more widespread, and in France, significant amounts of stock are held by the government. As **Figure 5** shows, the indexes that adjust for free

Table 4. Comparison of Europe Indexes

Description	MSCI Europe	FT/S&P-AWI	Salomon Brothers BMI
Number of stocks	574	718	1,824
Total capitalization (USD trillions)	2.9	3.4	4.0
Inception date	1969	1986	1989
Weighting method	Capitalization	Capitalization	Free float
Stock selection	Sampled	Sampled	All stocks
Minimum capitalization (USD millions)	—	100	Free float>100
Target capitalization capture	60%	81%	95%

Figure 4. Available Float

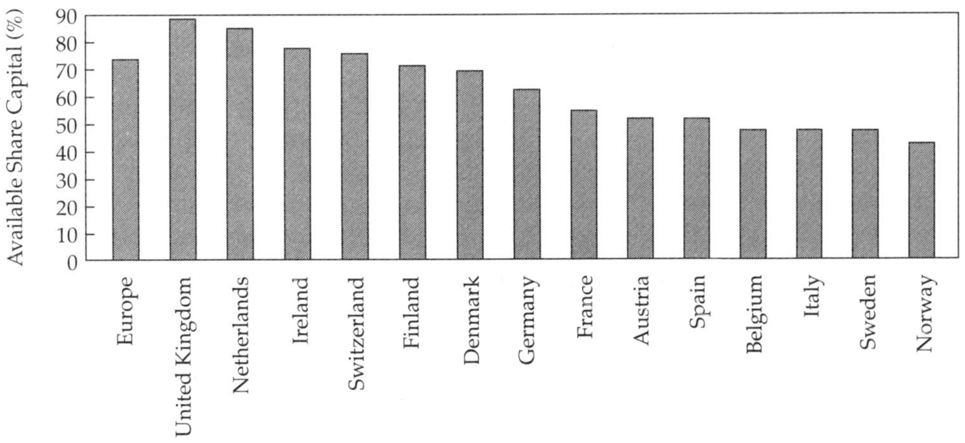

Figure 5. European Country Distribution

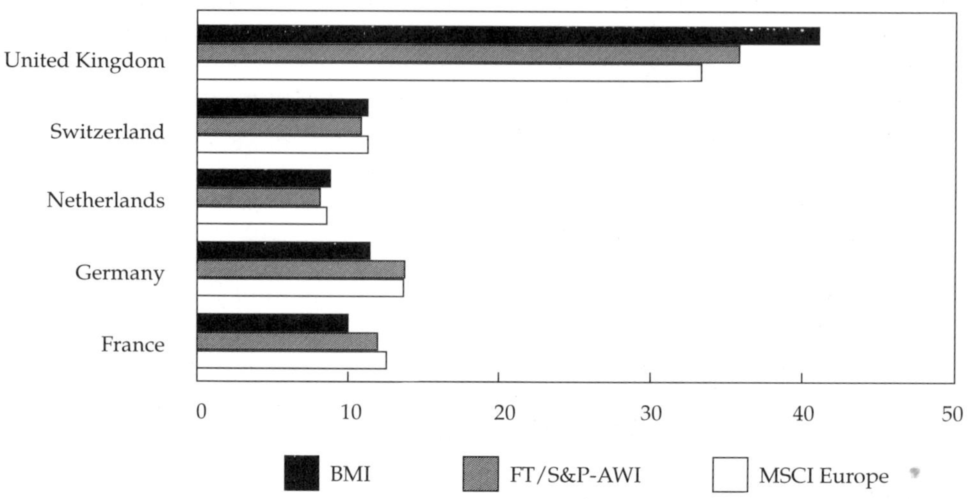

float, such as the Salomon BMI Index, include a heavier index weighting in the United Kingdom than in Germany or France because the United Kingdom has a high free float compared with other countries. A fund that wants to use a regional index, or on a broader basis, a global index, as a benchmark needs to know how cross-ownerships are handled in order to judge the suitability of index candidates.

PERFORMANCE ATTRIBUTION IN PRACTICE

Applying the performance attribution framework to a pension fund requires understanding the particulars of managing a pension fund: the pool of assets, the set of liabilities, and the goal of assuring that the return on the assets will meet present and future liabilities.

As a pension fund manager, we need to answer many questions in order to evaluate our decisions. Clearly, we need to know what the overall fund return is. We also need to know the value added by each of the managers for the fund: Does the added value justify the active-management fees we are paying? Does it meet the hurdle rate? How much effect do the major portfolio components have at the total fund level?

Materiality is also very important. We do not want to get bogged down in details, for example, by spending 50 percent of our time evaluating something that amounts to only 4 percent of the assets. Individual portfolio returns, whether they are in balanced or specialist portfolios, should be judged in terms of the value they add at the total fund level. If a rebalancing policy is in place, is it working? Are we rebalancing too often, not often enough? Are the ranges on either side of the target allocation too narrow or too wide? Does the fund hold too much cash? (The benchmark probably holds no cash.) How well is the fund doing relative to other funds in the marketplace? We may be happy to be underperforming other funds because we have a different liability structure. We may be happy that we have more in bonds, less in equities, and so forth, but we still need to know the reason for the underperformance.

Multilevel Analysis

The result of dealing with these strategic questions is the multilevel analytical process illustrated in **Figure 6**. Each question fits into one of the levels of this framework.

- *Total fund level*: At the top of the pyramid, the analysis focuses on how well the fund has done in aggregate and how its return compares with that of the strategic benchmark. This analysis is an acid test of how well the pension trustees have done and how the fund's performance relates to the decisions they made.
- *Broad asset-class level*: If the fund has a balanced manager at this level, it needs to evaluate how

Figure 6. Multilevel Analysis

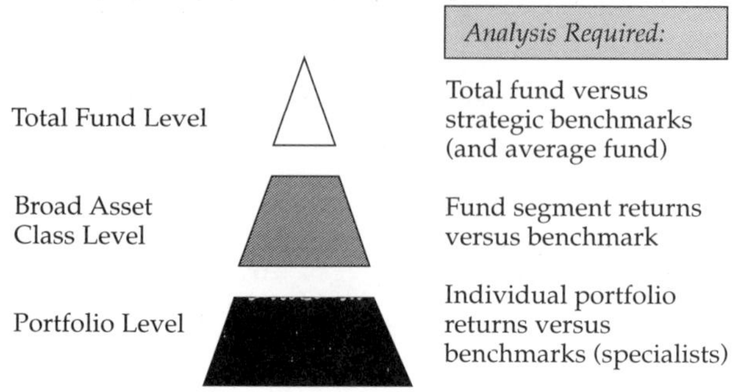

well that manager has done in asset allocation and in selection within the individual sectors and how much the aggregate has added in value.

- *Portfolio level*: The analysis required at this level involves the specialists managing the global portfolio, the domestic portfolio, currency, and so forth.

The value added at each level can be calculated and related back to the original decisions made within the investment process. Although the big-picture-level analysis does not specifically measure the currency effect, currency effects will be measured when we look at the individual managers and portfolios.

The strategic policy benchmark weights emerging from this analysis are shown in **Table 5**. The importance of this breakdown is that it shows that each benchmark weight in each broad segment of the fund (e.g., balanced managers) must relate to, first, the weight of the segment within the overall fund and, second, the total fund benchmark. Building a benchmark relationship like this is a little difficult, but it is essential to the effective measurement of the pension fund strategy using these techniques.

This basic approach can be related to the decisions a pension fund has to make: Which managers should it use? How should they be allocated across the fund? The structure shown is relatively complex, but this approach can be used to build a benchmark, consistent with any framework, that can be used to provide meaningful numbers for evaluating performance.

Practical issues may arise in using this approach. For example, individual managers may use different benchmarks for their portfolios than the fund uses for the total fund. At the total level, a U.K. pension fund may use the country components of the FT/S&P Actuaries World Index, but for the portion of the fund invested in the United States as a separate asset class, the benchmark might be the S&P 500. This difference might create a slight mismatch between the benchmarks at the total level and the individual asset-class levels, but the whole process generally works quite well. This example thus provides a useful instance of how you can apply theory in real life and receive some meaningful and useful answers.

Multilevel Decisions

Attribution theory naturally assumes that all decisions in a portfolio are made by comparing asset classes with one another directly. Such an approach might be thought of as a "single-level" analysis. In reality, however, allocation decisions may occur at more than one level. For example, a manager may start with a regional allocation (say, to overweight or underweight the Pacific Basin) and then make country-level allocation decisions within the region. This approach is quite valid and must be measured in a slightly different way. For example, a top-level decision to, say, overweight a region assumes implicitly that the index allocation has been adopted at this level. So, at the regional or top level, we can calculate an allocation effect and a currency effect based on the regional decision, but no security selection effects will occur. At the lower level, market returns will give rise to security selection effects, and the allocation and currency decisions will show the deviation from the index allocation within the block or region based on a secondary set of criteria.

In constructing an analysis to measure multilevel decisions, we must keep in mind that the return breakdown must provide real information about the portfolio in a way that is consistent with the decision-making process. **Table 6** shows the attribution breakdown for an unhedged U.S. dollar portfolio that is invested across Europe and the Pacific Basin. The portfolio outperformed by 1.85 percent. The analysis indicates that being overweight in Europe and underweight in the Pacific Basin was good in allocation terms but poor in currency terms. The overall effect of the currency decision overwhelmed the positive effect of allocation at Level 1, so the aggregate impact of the regional decision is negative. At Level 2, however, the picture is somewhat more encouraging. The

Table 5. Total Fund Level: Policy Benchmark Weights

	Type of Manager				
Asset	Balanced	Specialist	Index	Real Estate	Total
Manager-level allocation	30%	30%	30%	10%	100%
Equities	55	40	70	0	50
Bonds	15	30	0	0	14
North American equities	10	10	10	0	9
Pacific Basin equities	10	10	10	0	9
European equities	10	10	10	0	9
Real estate	0	0	0	100	10
Total	100%	100%	100%	100%	100%

Note: Numbers may not add to totals because of rounding.

Table 6. Return Breakdown by Region and Source of Return

Region	Level 1	Level 2
Europe	–0.21	0.33
Allocation	0.26	–0.04
Currency	–0.47	0.08
Selection	0.00	0.29
Pacific Basin	–0.44	2.17
Allocation	0.55	–0.01
Currency	–0.99	0.39
Selection	0.00	1.79
Total	–0.65	2.50

selection effects are positive (particularly in the Pacific Basin), and the aggregate impact of currency and allocation decision making relative to the benchmark is positive. This approach provides valuable insights into the investment process as it is actually carried out. Further, this analysis can be used to evaluate the approach itself, providing results that might not be forthcoming in a single-level analysis. For example, consistent evidence of negative currency and allocation effects at Level 1 might cast doubt on the decision process and could give rise to a reevaluation of the approach.

Bond Portfolios

Most of the performance attribution methodologies were developed to analyze equity portfolios. Nevertheless, many of the decisions in an equity strategy (e.g., currency exposure) are equally important for a bond portfolio. Applying a consistent approach across different types of portfolios is also worthwhile and useful. So, in my view, the standard attribution framework we have described works nearly as well for bonds as for equities. Some aspects of the approach work particularly well. For example, in a bond portfolio, currency decisions are particularly important and often make a larger contribution to total return than in equity portfolios; therefore, breaking down the components of currency return—hedging, the forward premium, and the currency-management effect—is helpful from a bond perspective.

This model is useful if the main decision for a global bond portfolio involves holding government bonds and allocating among individual markets and along the yield curve. We may increase duration in a particular market based on our view of interest rates, and we may over- or underweight among the markets based on how we think the individual market will perform relative to the world average. The selection effect becomes a combination of the duration decision, which is probably the most important, and sector and other (e.g., anomaly switching) effects within each market.

Using this approach for bond portfolios has certain weaknesses, however, because of the way some bond managers operate. For example, bond managers may not reallocate their assets among markets based on relative desirability of the market. Instead, they simply increase duration in one market and reduce duration in another. So, no "allocation" effect results, and the market preference will be reflected directly in the selection decision. Of course, the bottom line answer will be correct, but this attribution approach may not show the results strictly against the relevant attribution effect—that is, in the proper decision "bucket."

Figure 7 shows how we might adapt the typical equity framework of allocation, selection, and currency decisions to reflect the specialist factors in bond portfolios. This figure shows the allocation (assuming it is a separate decision), the duration and local country effects in each market (substituting for selection in the equity framework), and the currency effect (broken down as before). In attempting to extend this approach to a standard generic bond solution, the question is how to combine the allocation and duration effects in such a way as to meaningfully illustrate the investment process. The solution might simply be to combine the allocation and selection decisions. On balance, however, the described (ostensibly equity) approach adds considerable information and should be judged on its merits and not necessarily dismissed simply because it is less than perfect.

Figure 7. Attribution for Bonds

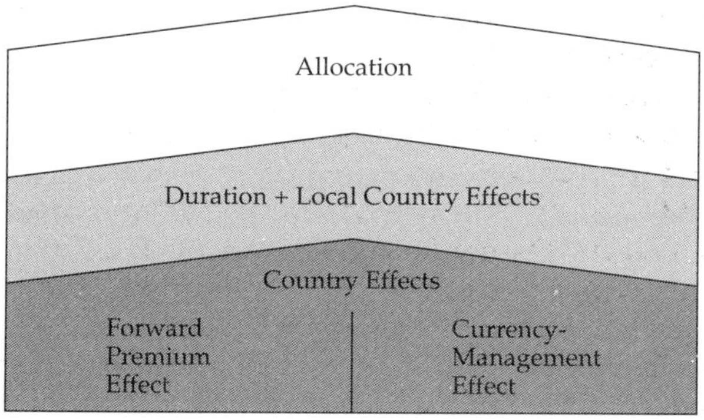

Additive versus Geometric Returns

The methodologies discussed so far essentially define the sum of the attribution effects as equal to the difference between the portfolio return and the benchmark return. In reality, however, cross-effects between currency and the local markets introduce small errors—which on occasion might not be that small. For example, the one-year total return for, say, a Swiss franc investor investing in the United States and earning a 10 percent U.S. dollar return and a 10 percent currency return will be 21 percent because of compounding. Using constantly compounded, or logarithmic, returns will overcome the question of what to do with the cross-term: the 1 percent that is unexplained by local market or currency return alone.

The alternative to additive attribution is the geometric approach, which essentially uses return relatives, reflects value added versus the benchmark, and allows for geometric linking over periods of time.[1] For short periods of time, attribution effects calculated under the geometric approach are the same as those using the additive approach, but over longer periods of time, they may be different. The geometric approach offers certain advantages. Using this method, attribution effects are the same regardless of the currency in which results are presented. Further, some practitioners claim that multiplicative attribution presents the portfolio excess return in a way that reflects the strength of the underlying benchmark. In other words, it recognizes that beating an index that has returned 50 percent is easier than beating an index that has returned 7 percent. The major difference between the additive and geometric approaches is demonstrated in **Table 7.** If the British pound benchmark return is 7 percent and the portfolio return in pounds is 10 percent, the portfolio outperformed in additive terms by 3 percent. Dividing the return relatives (i.e., 1.10/1.07) results in a multiplicative management effect of 2.8 percent. If these returns are converted into U.S. dollars, the additive attribution effects increase to 3.1 while the multiplicative effect (i.e., 1.122/1.091) remains the same. At higher rates of return, for example, a 53 percent portfolio return and a 50 percent benchmark return, the multiplicative approach further reduces the outperformance and expresses it in relative terms compared with the benchmark.

[1]AIMR Performance Presentation Standards require the use of time-weighted rates of return with valuation on at least a quarterly basis and geometric linking of period returns. See *AIMR Performance Presentation Standards Handbook,* 2nd ed. (Charlottesville, VA: AIMR, 1997).

CONCLUSION

Performance attribution is a useful management tool that provides feedback between portfolio managers and clients and evaluates value added in the decision-making process. An effective performance attribution framework is consistent with the decision-making process, reflects investors' objectives, and identifies both consistent superior performance and areas for improvement.

Single- and multicurrency attribution both decompose sources of return into the asset allocation effect and the security selection effect. Multicurrency attribution also captures the currency effect, including the effects of hedging, the forward premium, and the currency surprise.

Benchmarks should be clear, understandable, and unambiguous. They provide an objective test of whether a strategy was successfully implemented. Nevertheless, the discussion about an investment process often ignores the choice of a benchmark until the last moment, compromising performance results. Selecting the appropriate benchmark requires knowing how the various indexes are constructed. A comparison of European equity indexes demonstrates how benchmarks can differ—in number of stocks in the index, available history, weighting method, or selection criteria.

A multilevel analytical process addresses strategic performance questions and relates results back to the original decisions made within the investment process. Although bond portfolios are treated differently because the selection effect reflects duration and local market decisions, the multilevel decision approach can be applied for both global equity and global bond portfolios.

Performance attribution of global portfolios requires taking into account the cross-effects between currency and local markets. Although additive and geometric approaches produce the same returns over short periods of time, attribution results over longer periods of time may be different.

Table 7. Additive versus Multiplicative Return Effects

	Portfolio 1		Portfolio 2
Source of Return	GBP	USD	GBP
Portfolio	10.0	12.2	53.0
Index	7.0	9.1	50.0
Currency (USD)	2.0	0.0	2.0
Management effect (additive)	3.0	3.1	3.0
Management effect (multiplicative)	2.8	2.8	2.0

Question and Answer Session

John C. Stannard, CFA

Question: What about risk?

Stannard: The reason for not talking about risk is that it is such an enormous subject. Risk is extremely important. A committee meeting set up under the jurisdiction of the European Federation of Financial Analyst Societies looked at this whole question of attribution, particularly focusing on bonds. Roughly one-third of the time was allocated to discussing the subject of risk, but no one agreed about anything except that risk is important. Proponents of different approaches often favor a particular risk measure—volatility, the Sharpe measure, or some other. Risk is different things to different people, but it must be interpreted in terms of the goals and objectives of the portfolio. The portfolio and benchmark returns are comparable only if the risk levels are similar.

Question: Don't you need to have the exchange rate that is used for any big transaction to assess the currency effect; for example, don't you require a daily accounting system?

Stannard: Yes. Most people approach this problem by bringing their portfolios back to a base currency. I take into account the exchange rate on the day of the transaction and the benefit that accrued in the base currency at that time. If I am in a particular market and either come out of the market completely halfway through the period or double my weighting, then the effect could actually be greater than the differences in exchange rates. The time horizon in which you analyze these things is important. AIMR has addressed this issue for performance measurement, but time horizon is more important in performance attribution.[1] We would like to adjust for exchange rates on a daily basis, but in reality, daily adjustment is difficult, particularly when you have to collect index data and balance them every day. Most of the time, the adjustment is probably quite reasonably done monthly, provided no massive swings occur.

[1]See *AIMR Performance Presentation Standards Handbook* (1997).

Question: If empirical evidence indicates that aggregate past performance is not predictive, except for descriptive purposes, why use performance attribution?

Stannard: As a manager, you are much more likely to get an assignment if you have good performance than if you have poor performance. As a buyer of investment management services, you must analyze not only the performance of a particular firm but also the way it makes its decisions, whether it can retain its staff, and so forth. You must understand whether a particular investment process actually works and whether it will continue to work. If you blindly accept an attribution analysis and assume performance will be the same in the future, you could be wrong. Nevertheless, in conjunction with understanding investment managers and the investment process, attribution analysis provides good information on which to base future decisions.

Post-EMU Bond Markets

Stefan Laternser
Chief of Bond Research
Bank Julius Baer

Upon advent of the European Monetary Union, credit analysis will be *the* paramount issue in European fixed-income research. EMU participants will relinquish the right to issue debt in their own currency, and structured products will develop, which highlights the growing importance of instrument-risk management. The prime catalyst for the development of new products in Europe will be declining profit margins and competition brought on by the EMU. Adding value in the post-EMU era will require an expanded knowledge base—economics to assess sovereign risk, accounting and fundamental analysis to analyze credit risk, and financial theory to understand instrument risk.

The European Monetary Union (EMU) will create a huge bond market in a single currency, the euro. The advent of this market will dramatically change the way bond analysts and portfolio managers conduct their businesses and create value. Credit-risk management will take center stage in the era ahead, and instrument-risk management will have secondary but increasing importance. Compared with 10 years ago, the high-yielding markets in Europe have vanished to a large extent, compelling a shift in focus when investing in Europe and creating new challenges for European bond analysts and portfolio managers.

This presentation provides an overview of the new euro market and the new strategies that will evolve and replace traditional European fixed-income strategies. It also estimates the impact of the EMU on credit ratings and credit spreads of new euro debt issues, underscores the primary importance of credit-risk analysis with the advent of the EMU, and discusses the increasing importance of managing instrument risk and structuring prepayment risk. The EMU will be the primary catalyst for the development of a structured products market in Europe.

THE EURO MARKET

With broad participation in the EMU, the euro market—which includes treasury, agency, corporate, and high-yield bonds, as well as asset-backed securities (ABS)—will amount to about USD7.6 trillion outstanding as of 1996, or about 37 percent of the world bond market. It will be comparable in size to the U.S. bond market, which currently stands at about USD8.8 trillion outstanding and accounts for 43 percent of the world bond market, as shown in **Table 1**.

A comparison of the composition of the euro and U.S. bond markets, as shown in **Figure 1**, indicates that some segments of the euro market will be as developed as the U.S. market and other segments will not be as developed or do not currently exist. For example, with USD3.5 trillion outstanding, the euro central government bond market will be much larger than that of the United States, but the U.S. agency and agency-guaranteed market and state and local government markets will be significantly larger than comparable segments within the euro market.

The major dimensions to bond investment risk are interest rate risk, credit risk, option and prepayment risk, and currency risk. The major risks in European bond markets currently are interest rate and currency. For example, investors in high-yielding markets, such as Italy, Spain, and Greece, have been confronted with high interest rate and currency risks, which can be extremely costly if not properly managed. Because the euro market will be so new, credit ratings will be of paramount importance to investors.

The popularity of traditional strategies will diminish with the loss of 14 currencies and 14 yield curves in the post-EMU period and will be reduced to a pure interest rate strategy for euro portfolios. This strategy combines modification of portfolio duration, depending on the interest rate outlook,

Table 1. Characteristics of the Eurobond and the U.S. Bond Markets, 1996

	Europe	United States	World
Outstanding (USD billions)	$7,630	$8,837	$20,483
Share of world market	37.3%	43.1%	100.0%
Rating (average)	Aa1/AA+	Aaa/AAA	na
Sovereign ceiling	Aaa/AAA	Aaa/AAA	na

na = not applicable.

Sources: Bank Julius Baer, Salomon Brothers, Moody's, and Standard & Poor's data.

with yield curve strategies—creating exposure to different segments of the yield curve. It also means picking up high-quality bonds that offer relative value, selling "expensive" bonds, and buying "cheap" bonds.

Other strategies will evolve. First, European investors will diversify *vertically*, staying within Europe but diversifying into lower quality credits—quasi-sovereign, corporate, asset-backed, high-yield, and distressed bonds. Second, investors in Europe will expand their universe *horizontally* by investing in emerging market sovereign risk in hard-currency markets, through Brady bonds, or investing in newly emerging currency markets, such as South Africa. Third, investors will focus on option and prepayment risk instruments—ABS, mortgage-backed securities (MBS), and other structured products—to enhance total return. Effective vertical and horizontal diversification will make credit risk the focal point for fixed-income analysis.

EUROPEAN SOVEREIGN-RISK MANAGEMENT

Bond analysts, portfolio managers, and investors will focus a lot of attention on credit-risk analysis and sovereign-risk management, analyzing the credit ratings and credit spreads of EMU members. With the advent of the EMU, member-government bonds and the governments themselves will lose their sovereign-risk status because participants will relinquish the right to print money and to service debt in a non-EMU currency. The Maastricht Treaty has a "no-bail-out" clause, so if a country such as Italy, one of the largest debtors, defaults on its euro obligations, investors cannot assume that the European Community will bail out the financially distressed country. Only the advent of political union after monetary union takes place will create generic euro sovereign risk comparable to that of U.S. Treasury securities.

Sovereign Credit Ratings

The credit-rating agencies have different philosophies for rating new euro debt issues. Loss of sovereign risk status and the no-bail-out clause have major implications for credit ratings. According to Standard & Poor's Corporation and International Bank Credit Analyst (IBCA), domestic debt effectively becomes foreign debt with the loss of monetary sovereignty,

Figure 1. Composition of European and U.S. Bond Markets, 1996

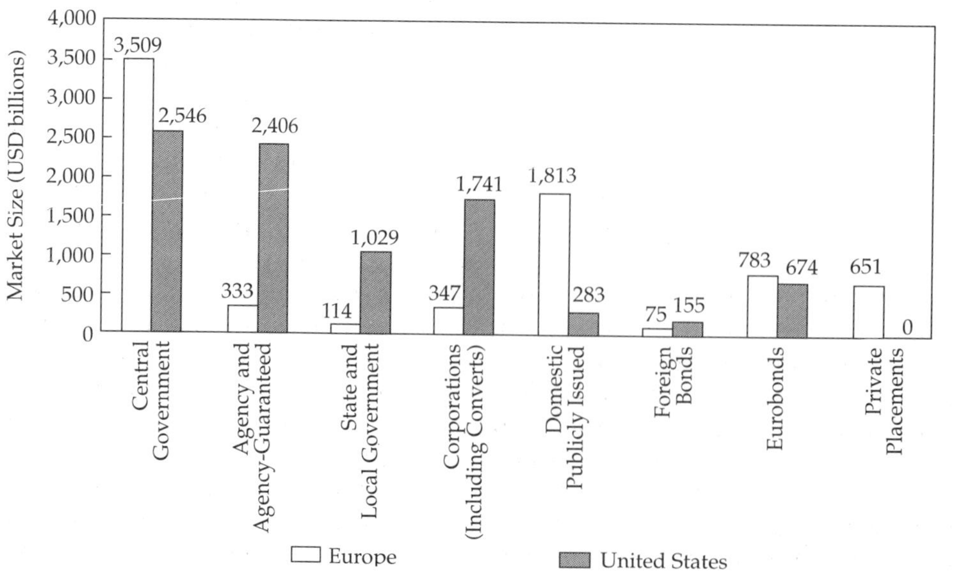

Source: Based on JBcoB and Salomon Brothers data.

and therefore, foreign debt ratings will apply. Moody's Investors Service has a slightly different and more complicated approach: On the EMU start date, Moody's rating of each member's domestic debt will become that government's rating for the debt denominated in euro. Based on the new rating philosophies, the euro market will be initially rated, on average, only Aa1/AA+. An interesting implication of this initial credit rating is that interest rate swaps could trade through some government bond yields. If credit risk for a given government is rising, interest rate swaps, which have a better credit rating than the respective government bonds, could trade at a lower yield.

Credit Spreads

Not surprisingly, specific EMU government issues will also have different spreads. **Table 2** provides results from a Bank Julius Baer (JBcoB) poll that surveyed brokerage houses for possible post-EMU spread levels among EMU participants. The poll indicates, for example, that Germany and France would have spread levels ranging from 0 to 10 basis points, depending on which country will have the effective euro benchmark bond. Belgium would trade at 10–60 basis points over the benchmark—remarkable for a country that is already assumed by the bond markets to be in monetary union. Although some markets, such as Ireland and Finland, would have tight spread levels (at 10–25 basis points), countries such as Italy would have wider spread levels (at 40–80 basis points).

Table 2. Possible Post-EMU Spread Levels

Country	Spread
France	0–10
Germany	0–10
Netherlands	0–10
Denmark	0–25
Finland	10–25
Ireland	10–25
Spain	10–25
United Kingdom	10–35
Belgium	10–60
Italy	40–80

A country's economic situation, its budget situation, and the size of its overall debt burden drive credit spreads, which helps explain the wide spreads in Italy and Belgium. Although those countries' debt loads and shares of world debt burden have not been much of a problem, their economic and fiscal situations need improvement. Some countries, such as Italy, Belgium, and emerging markets, can more easily make a market for their debt in local currencies than in foreign currency because they are the prime debtors in their currencies. The no-bail-out clause makes it difficult for banks to indiscriminately lend their money to their former sovereign debtors without seeking a higher credit spread.

Investors also require wider spreads to compensate for higher perceived risk. For example, although Belgium has a significant yield premium, Italy is a riskier play because of its turbulent political and economic history. The United Kingdom, which does not belong to continental Europe, has a fairly wide spread level because of the opt-out clause—the possibility to stay out of the EMU but enter whenever the U.K. wishes to do so. Also, its economic risk is perceived to be large because its economy is strongly linked to the U.S. economic cycle.

Market structure characteristics—issuance, transparency, liquidity, and market breadth—also affect spreads. Because of its transparent market structure and established repo and zero-coupon markets, France could take over the benchmark function. In this case, France's credit spread would be zero and German euro issues could trade at a spread above French euro issues. Germany, however, is committed to market reforms that will make its market more transparent than it is now. Although a huge overall euro market will develop, a market much bigger than the U.S. Treasury market, the liquidity of the euro market may not be as great as many investors think. The overall market size, about USD3.5 trillion, will not drive bid–ask spreads, but the relative size of each tranche and selective issues will. No component of the euro market is bigger than the U.S. Treasury market, which may have a surprising impact on liquidity.

CREDIT-RISK MANAGEMENT

The credit-risk universe comprises four elements:

- Corporate default risk, which is probably the most commonly known and evaluated element of credit risk.
- Country risk, which is more common in emerging markets than in others and must be analyzed and managed differently from corporate risk.
- Collateral risk, which will present European investors with a new kind of risk as the ABS market grows. Collateral risk arises from the bundling of assets—for example, credit card balances and mortgages—into large pools of assets. The ABS market offers a good credit risk for a relatively high return and can solve a lot of the problems in Europe and Japan, but it does pose underlying collateral risk.
- Instrument risk, which is exposure to credit options, prepayment options, structured notes, or derivative instruments.

Properties of Credit Risk

Credit risk is the possibility that a debtor will default and not pay its liabilities in full when due. Research on credit risk has raised several points worth keeping in mind:

- Credit risk is best captured in a credit rating. Moody's default rates for Aaa-rated to B-rated bonds over the 1972–92 period, as shown in **Figure 2**, confirm that higher default rates are reflected in dramatically lower credit ratings.
- Defaults are a function of time. Bonds can experience secular credit deterioration, or ratings drift, over time. **Table 3** shows average letter-rating changes for two-year and five-year transition periods. For example, over the 1920–95 period, only 79.7 percent of Aaa-rated bonds remained Aaa rated and 9.5 percent drifted downward to a Aa rating; over the 1920–92 period, only 60.8 percent of Aaa-rated bonds remained Aaa rated, 15.2 percent were downgraded to Aa, and more than 18.0 percent were downgraded below a B rating. An interesting observation from Table 3 is the asymmetry that exists with respect to credit ratings—more firms experience downgrades than upgrades.
- Credit seasoning affects default rates through time, as illustrated in **Figure 3**. For example, B-rated bonds initially have fairly high default rates, which decrease over time. By the 11th year, the default rate of B-rated bonds is comparable to or better than that of Ba-rated bonds and offers investors a better risk/return trade-off.
- Default rates vary over the business cycle. Annual default rates since 1970 for speculative and investment-grade bonds, shown in **Figure 4**, highlight how the credit cycle tracks the business cycle. Default rates increase during economic downturns, such as the recession of 1990 and 1991. As the economy improves, default rates decline, as they did in 1992. Thus, managing the credit cycle provides another opportunity to add value through active management. For example,

Figure 2. Default Rates and Credit Ratings

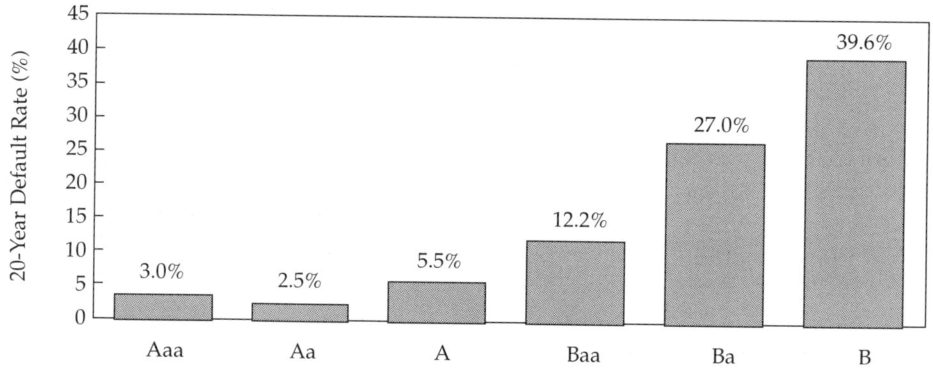

Source: Based on Moody's data.

Table 3. Rating Transition Matrixes

	Later Rating						
Initial Rating	Aaa	Aa	A	Baa	Ba	B	Other
Two-Year Average Rating Transition Matrix, 1920–95							
Aaa	79.70%	9.51%	2.01%	0.45	0.15	0.01%	8.16%
Aa	2.00	76.26	9.5	1.43	0.42	0.03	10.36
A	0.10	3.77	75.79	7.17	1.28	0.22	11.66
Baa	0.05	0.42	6.42	69.73	6.71	1.29	15.38
Ba	0.03	0.14	0.74	7.5	63.73	7.06	20.80
B	0.00	0.05	0.23	1.18	8.63	60.42	29.49
Five-Year Average Rating Transition Matrix, 1920–92							
Aaa	60.78	15.21	4.33	0.96	0.49	0.09	18.13
Aa	3.43	54.14	15.93	3.42	1.16	0.20	21.72
A	0.20	5.85	55.74	10.34	2.58	0.69	24.59
Baa	0.09	0.92	10.01	47.06	8.03	2.00	31.88
Ba	0.04	0.26	1.92	10.40	36.48	8.09	42.81
B	0.02	0.09	0.48	2.41	10.25	32.12	54.63

Source: Moody's.

Figure 3. Credit Seasoning Effect: Probability of Default in Future Years

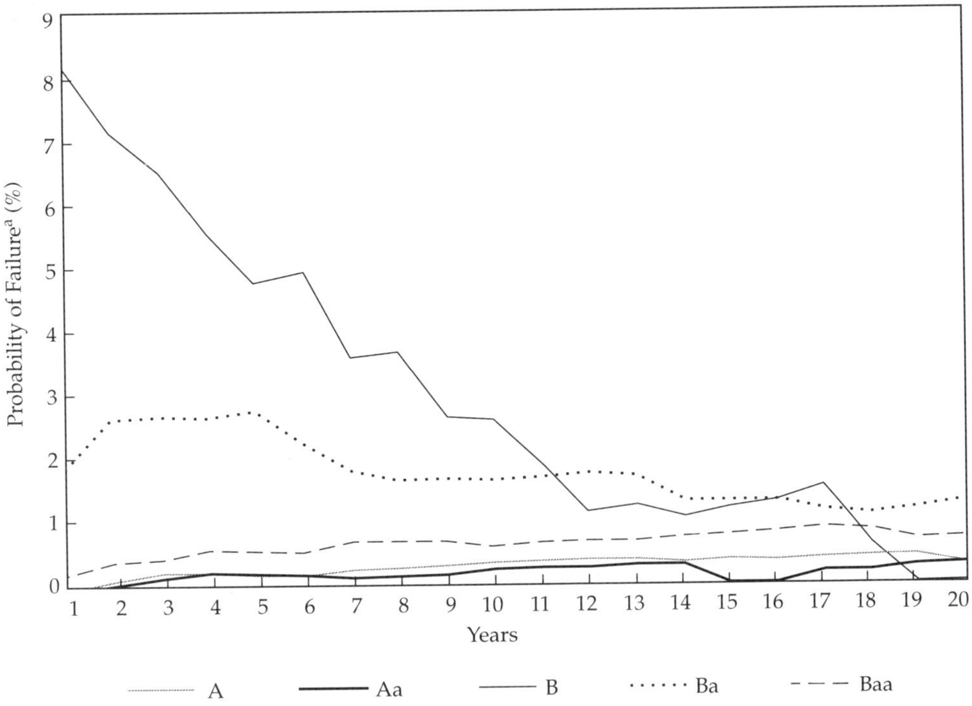

[a]Probability that a corporation with rating *r* will default in year *n* based on 1972–92 experience.

Source: Based on Moody's data.

if the economy is expected to deteriorate, switching back into treasuries or "flight to quality" will add value.

- Loss severity is a function of the business cycle and the seniority of the creditor's claim. Recovery rates on defaulted bonds should be analyzed in two dimensions—the business cycle and the seniority structure. **Table 4** shows that average recovery rates are lower for subordinate or junior levels of debt and during economic downturns. For example, recovery rates for senior secured debt in 1991 were about 60 percent of par value, compared with about 17 percent for subordinated debt. To the advantage of investors, a distressed bond trades at about 20 percent of par value in a good environment, well below the weighted-average recovery rate of 40 percent.
- The greater the credit risk, the greater the

Figure 4. Default Rates by Investment Grade, 1970–92

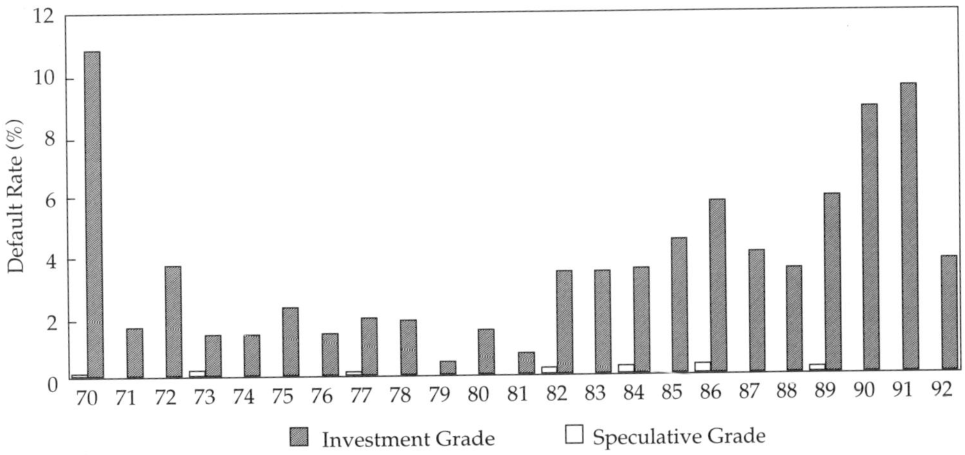

Source: Based on Moody's data.

Table 4. Average Price Recovery Rates of Different Asset Classes

Debit Class	1974–92	1992	1991	1990	1989	1988
Senior secured	66.8%	59.2%	60.8%	33.7%	74.6%	76.3%
Senior unsecured	47.3	51.1	45.5	35.3	43.3	44.6
Senior subordinated	32.9	50.1	33.7	26.5	40.3	39.9
Subordinated	28.0	47.3	16.6	23.4	26.0	35.0
Junior subordinated	18.0	NA	3.6	18.9	17.5	3.6
Weighted average	40.0	50.5	32.7	28.2	39.1	44.3

NA = not available.

Source: Moody's.

required yield. As shown in **Figure 5,** investors seeking higher yields must assume greater credit risk. Spreads to U.S. Treasury securities for Baa-rated bonds are significantly higher than those for Aaa-rated bonds—more than 800 basis points during the 1982 recession.

Privatization in Europe

Looking at European credit ratings and ownership structure, credit risk does not appear to be a problem, but a paradigm change will occur. Philosophically, citizens relied heavily on the state to provide many services—mail, telecommunications, and infrastructure—not realizing that the market is a more efficient tool for allocating these services at the best cost with great transparency. Governments simply cannot afford to hold on to state companies or subsidize jobs at any cost, because budget constraints are too strong and the costs of mistakes made in the early 1990s are overwhelming. As a result, more government-controlled companies, such as European utilities and state services (Post, Bahn, and Telecom, for example) will be privatized and lose their sovereign or agency status. Although they may remain "too big to fail," their credit ratings could be much lower than that of a typical government entity, providing an opportunity to pick up additional yield as credit ratings change.

The long-term outlook may not be negative, but it requires more-selective evaluation of sovereigns and corporates on a stand-alone basis. Sovereign guarantees will be removed, special mandates will be phased out, and monopolies will be abolished. Markets will open up, competition will increase, and regulations will be relaxed. A downgrade may also occur if competitors with low ratings take over highly rated privatized companies. Other threats to bondholders are *altlasten*—the German euphemism for the monetary value of all mistakes and liabilities that have accumulated in the balance sheet over time—and shareholder value. A reduction in equity reduces the risk cushion available to bondholders, increasing corporate risk, credit risk, and the likelihood of a downgrade. As a result, bondholders will suffer because the bonds suddenly carry a higher yield.

Investors can reduce risk by effectively analyzing companies on a bond-by-bond basis. Distinguishing between explicit (stated) guarantees, moral guarantees, and stand-alone ratings versus structured product ratings is important. Simply because a company

Figure 5. Yield and Credit Risk

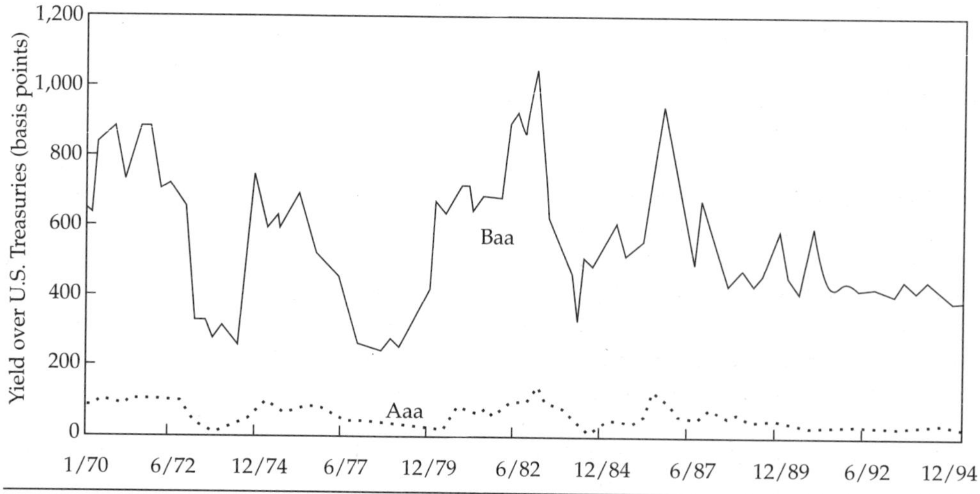

Source: Based on Moody's data.

has a strong name—for example Europäische Hypothekenbank (EHB), also known as the European Mortgage Bank—does not mean it is state guaranteed. A well-known issuer in the German Pfandbriefe (mortgage bond) market, Deutsche Pfandbriefbank, also known as the German Mortgage Bank or Depfa, receives two ratings: the Aaa/AAA rating as the rating for Pfandbriefe and a Aa3 rating as its stand-alone credit rating. Even a company that is "too big to fail" does not automatically imply a strong rating or prevent a downgrade. That description may help to market such a bond to a customer, but the company can still be downgraded.

In the end, credit analysis is *the* important issue in European fixed-income research. Some firms have already taken the appropriate measures by hiring people who know how to evaluate companies—not economists, but auditors and accountants.

Credit Risk and Portfolio Management

Although credit risk can be very challenging for portfolio managers, a few pointers can help simplify it. First, like watching the business cycle, watch the credit cycle and its movements. Second, follow country and company news. From this point of view, bond analysis will become similar to fundamental equity analysis in which investors, rather than looking purely at interest rates, analyze financial statements, especially balance sheets, and draw investment implications. Credit risk is "balance sheets and bottom line." Third, as in quality switching or intermarket spread swaps, select a desirable credit-rating range. For example, depending on the economic environment, non-risk-averse investors may shift from BBB-rated to B-rated bonds in an improving or expanding economy to capture higher yields in exchange for the additional risk. Fourth, choose an acceptable maturity range for lower quality credits. The greater the exposure to longer duration assets, the greater the financial hit if credit deteriorates. Fifth, consider the portfolio approach for particular clients. For example, do not expose private clients to a single bond but select an appropriate portfolio of bonds or a bond fund.

Development of New Market Segments

As a result of monetary union, new segments of the European bond market similar to the seasoned U.S. bond market will develop, creating new opportunities for portfolio managers and investors. Instead of financing through the central government, municipal entities will come to the market and finance themselves. Valuable opportunities will develop in structured products, although deal structures will probably not be as complicated as U.S. structured products. The EMU will also give rise to corporate investment-grade, high-yield, and distressed securities. Alongside these new opportunities, the Eurobond market will continue to function as an offshore market, although not in Deutsche marks or French francs, but in newly emerging currencies, such as the Czech krona, the South African rand, or the Korean won.

INSTRUMENT-RISK MANAGEMENT

Managing the risk associated with new financial products is a challenging task that requires a totally different approach in order to deal with structural risk and option and prepayment risk. ABS, including MBS, offer customized credit risk and prepayment features so that a fairly solid structure can be created from pools of assets.

Structured Products

Structured products are customized products designed to replicate synthetically the returns in different markets. These products have unlimited possibilities in global fixed-income markets. **Figure 6** illustrates the mechanics of structured products and how investors can easily gain synthetic exposure to different asset classes. These instruments are structured by combining a floating- or fixed-rate bond with a derivative instrument to achieve the desired payout. For example, investors can take leveraged or unleveraged interest rate views by using off-balance-sheet transactions (e.g., interest rate swaps), enhance yield by using options, take yield curve views by using collared floaters, or take credit views by using credit options. Structured products can also create exposure to other assets, such as commodities or stock indexes, and most importantly, they can isolate risk via put options, swaptions, caps, collars, or floors.

The value of a structured product equals its break-up value, or the sum of the hedged components. Volatility, strike rates, short-term interest rates, underlying yields or term structure, order flow, liquidity, and level of structure complexity affect the valuation of structured products.

ABS, a rapidly growing segment of the structured products market, are used to securitize and effectively liquidate assets—mortgages, credit card receivables, default receivables, bank loans, and so forth. They can solve many of the problems international banks face, including cleaning up their balance sheets. ABS are highly flexible and combine collateral characteristics (e.g., call risk, prepayment risk, and credit risk) with structural characteristics (e.g., early amortization, clean-up calls, and credit enhancements). For example, ABS permit structuring of credit risk—engineering a credit rating—and transferring of prepayment risk, as with MBS and collateralized

Figure 6. Mechanics of Structured Products

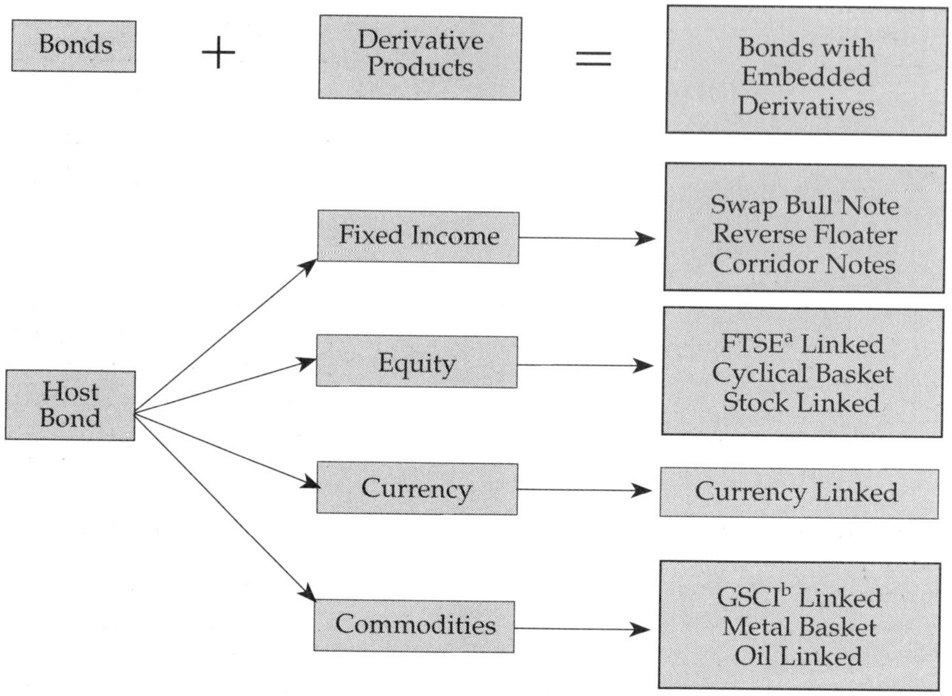

[a]Financial Times/Standard & Poor's Actuaries World Index.

[b]Goldman Sachs Commodity Index.

mortgage obligations (CMOs). ABS also offer fairly stable ratings, AAA-rated to C-rated paper, and attractive yields.

Although credit risk is difficult to hedge, it can be structured through ABS, as **Table 5** shows. Cash flows from the underlying pool are sliced and directed to different tranches with payment priorities that depend on the credit rating. The top tranche or senior tranche carries the highest rating—typically Aaa—and receives cash flows first and in full. The remaining cash flows are used to pay down the subordinate tranches. If the underlying pool experiences principal losses, defaults, or bankruptcies, cash flows will not be sufficient to serve all tranches, and the most junior subordinate class bears any cash flow shortfalls—Tranche G in this example. If the capital protection of Tranche G is consumed, Tranche F will bear further credit losses and so forth. This structuring technique has a cushion effect—losses have to exceed the size of the cushion before the senior tranche experiences any losses. This cushion, 6 percent in this example, is distributed among the junior tranches with the lowest rated tranche having the smallest cushion. In the event of extensive credit losses, mechanisms such as early amortization further protect the senior class.

Table 5. Structuring Credit Risk

Class	Rating	Class Size	Size of Cushion
A	AAA/AA	94.0%	6.0%
B	AA	2.0	4.0
C	A	1.0	3.0
D	BBB	1.0	2.0
E	BB	1.0	1.0
F	B	0.5	0.5
G	Unrated	0.5	0.0

Although ABS can earn high yields, the structure of these instruments gets highly complex, requiring analysts to do some extra homework—analyzing the collateral, structure, tools, and the bond. Collateral must be analyzed for credit risk and prepayment projections. The entire structure must be analyzed to understand the credit and prepayment protection of each tranche. The tools or instruments used must be analyzed; for example, fixed-rate U.S. dollar collateral swapped into floating-rate German marks requires counterparty risk analysis. The final stage is bond analysis in terms of credit, duration, and convexity. Premium yields for ABS are not a free lunch; they are the price for due diligence work.

Compared with corporate bonds, MBS and other ABS show remarkable credit-rating stability, very good credits, and relatively high yields. As **Table 6** indicates, the possibility of structuring a credit rating and multiple built-in cushions leads to fewer credit-rating downgrades than for corporate bonds.

Table 6. Rating Stability

	1991		1992	
Bond Type	Upgrade	Downgrade	Upgrade	Downgrade
Corporate	13.3%	37.6%	12.1%	36.3%
Mortgage-backed security	3.4	0.8	9.4	3.7
Collateral	3.4	0.5	9.4	2.9
Structure	0.0	0.3	0.0	0.8

Source: Moody's.

MBS and CMOs are a totally different ball game; the object of this investment is not structuring credit risk but structuring prepayment risk. Because of the complex combination of different kinds of embedded options, MBS and CMOs are probably the wildest animals in the fixed-income arena. Because of the option to prepay at any time, the mortgagor influences the price of MBS, but exercise of the prepayment option is not always rational or efficient; for example, a good supply of Government National Mortgage Association (GNMA) 11 percent coupon MBS is available—well above current coupon MBS—which have not prepayed. MBS are also path dependent, which alters their price and risk characteristics.

Structuring prepayment risk in MBS is similar to structuring credit risk in any other ABS. Certain tranches absorb the brunt of prepayments, and other tranches have more stable cash flows. The interacting behavior of cash flow absorbers, known as companion or support tranches, and cash flow protected tranches, known as planned amortization classes (PACs), has to be analyzed carefully and tested vigorously, using scenario techniques and simulations. **Figure 7** illustrates the dynamic behavior of MBS, showing how support tranches protect the principal cash flows and average lives of PACs with wide prepayment bands—Tranches G and H. Classes D, C, E, and F sequentially absorb all prepayments before G and H experience any principal amortization.

The price of absorbing the prepayment risk for PAC tranches is higher yields. **Table 7** shows that under different average-life assumptions, spreads to Treasuries for companion and support classes are significantly higher than the PAC classes. For example, using a four-year average life assumption, the yield over the 10-year Treasury for a companion tranche is 295 basis points versus only 65 basis points for a PAC tranche.

MBS fare best in an environment of low or decreasing volatility because the straddle-position MBS represent profits from falling volatility. **Figure 8** indicates the most appropriate MBS investments under alternative yield and volatility scenarios. For example, under declining interest rates and volatility, current-coupon and discount MBS passthroughs offer the highest yields. Thus, MBS and CMOs are the most complex instruments in the fixed-income arena because prepayments are never known with certainty. Although the prepayment risk can be modified by structuring, it can never be tamed.

Figure 7. Dynamic Behavior of CMOs

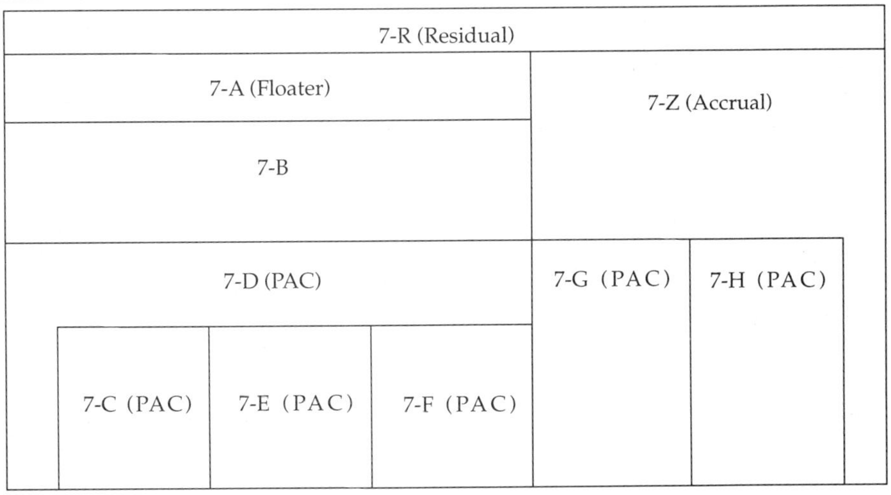

Table. 7 The Price of Prepayment Risk: Spread over 10-Year Treasury, by Tranche Type
(basis points)

Average Life (years)	PAC	Sequential	PAC II	LIBOR Floater	Companion
2	53	120	180	25	400
3	60	120	200	35	350
4	65	125	190	45	295
5	75	125	185	60	250
6	78	120	160	80	195
10	74	120	135	100	155
20	73	105	100	125	90

Note: Spreads based on GNMA MBS initially priced at 95 basis points over 10-year Treasury.
Source: Bloomberg.

Figure 8. Yield–Volatility Expectations

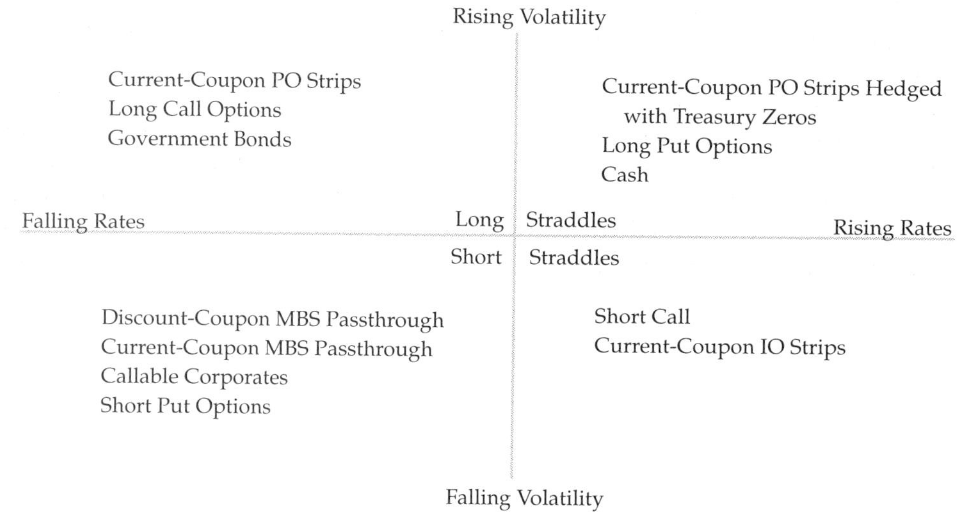

SOVEREIGN HIGH-YIELD MARKETS

Sovereign high-yield markets are a source of horizontal credit diversification because traditional European high yielders (such as "Club Med" bonds of Italy, Spain, Portugal, and Greece) have seen a convergence in yields over the past two years. Investors interested in high-yield markets will look to regions such as Latin America or Eastern Europe, where sound economic policies and a relatively stable political environment should fuel convergence in currencies and interest rates, as demonstrated dramatically in Italy in 1996. Emerging market debt in hard currencies, such as the U.S. dollar or German mark, as well as in local currencies, offers potential if the countries follow the right economic and fiscal policies. Thus, value can be extracted from proper economic research and traditional European bond market analysis.

The bond market for emerging countries can be divided into two segments: bonds in hard currency (for example, Brady bonds) and in local currency. The development and the effects that were tied to the Brady bond market brought emerging market bonds to investors' attention. After a host of Latin American countries defaulted on their commercial bank loans, a Brady exchange—named after then Secretary of the U.S. Treasury, Nicholas Brady—was proposed to solve the problems of soured U.S. bank exposure in these countries and their inability to develop their economies following strict reform policies in exchange for partial debt forgiveness. The success of the Brady markets and the reforms in the respective countries led to the development of local markets. Local currency markets are especially well developed in Southeast Asia, with Latin America and eastern Europe making strong progress. These markets exhibit a significant degree of credit, interest rate, and currency risk and, therefore, warrant careful research and risk management.

CONCLUSION

With broad participation in the EMU, the European bond market will be comparable in size to the U.S. bond market and the European government market segment will be larger than the U.S. Treasury market. As the euro debt market evolves, size, composition, liquidity, and credit ratings will change.

New strategies will evolve in the post-EMU era as European investors diversify vertically into lower quality credits and horizontally into other currencies, highlighting the central importance of credit-risk analysis. Sovereign high-yield markets provide both a source of horizontal diversification and a way to add value using traditional bond market analysis. Although initial credit ratings, on average, for EMU members will be Aa1/AA+, credit ratings and spread levels for specific EMU government issues will be determined by a country's economic situation, debt load, percentage of world debt, perceived risk, and market structure. Investors and portfolio managers should be mindful of the properties of credit ratings when making fixed-income investments, because credit risk is best captured in a credit rating.

New products, such as ABS, will help banks clean up their balance sheets and offer investors relatively high yields, but these products will require a strong understanding of instrument risk. ABS and MBS issuers can structure credit and prepayment risk, allowing investors to select attractive classes based on their risk preferences. Premium yields on structured products are the reward for due diligence work and for understanding the collateral, structure, tools, and the bond itself.

The profile of the European bond analyst will change dramatically and involve three important skills: a traditional economic background to apply economic models and to analyze traditional European sovereign markets, a strong accounting background to complete fundamental analysis and credit-risk assessments of specific entities in the post-EMU era, and a mathematical or theoretical background to analyze the structures of ABS and MBS with embedded options, derivatives, and prepayment features. These skills address the key risks—sovereign risk, credit risk, and instrument risk—facing bond investors in the post-EMU era. Understanding these risks will become much more important in the future for portfolio managers and bond analysts, because the more you know about risk, the easier it is to add value.

Question and Answer Session

Stefan Laternser

Question: Will the size of the euro market grow and will that growth provide the required liquidity?

Laternser: Yes, I believe that market will grow and will be a source of liquidity, but it will need to resemble the U.S. Treasury market. Although the current European market is less liquid than the U.S. Treasury market, it will improve and we will see larger issues that will provide better liquidity. For example, recently, German *Laender* (federal states), instead of individually issuing small amounts of securities, collectively issued a DEM4 billion bond.

Question: Do you believe corporate spreads will be tied to home-country spreads?

Laternser: No, because rating agencies and credit analysts will look at companies on a stand-alone basis. If a company is judged to be of AAA quality, it should trade at AAA levels—which country it comes from is not important. If an Italian company is better than a German company, the Italian company will have the lower spreads. If you are the first one to adopt the rigid criteria and apply it to value, you will realize and capture this value, for example, by switching into Italian AAA debt.

With a sovereign ceiling, a Spanish company, for example, could issue AAA-rated ABS, although the Spanish government's rating is only Aa2. We will have to become accustomed to this idea. A different situation exists in Mexico. For example, if a German company is located in Mexico, the currency-risk problem is still there, but for Italy, Germany, and other euro market companies, the currency will be the same. Because country risk and currency risk are primarily the same, the country risk will diminish.

Question: Will new rating agencies emerge as a result of the development of the new euro debt market?

Laternser: New rating agencies could emerge, but because Moody's, S&P, and even IBCA are established companies in this field, a new company would have to produce a lot of convincing work or genuine new ideas to establish itself in the market. The recent merger of IBCA and Fitch Investors Service indicates that ratings are also a size "business"—that is, it takes a critical size to survive in this market. I rely strongly on established rating agencies, but I also rely on independent sources such as those already published by well-known investment banks, because the major rating agencies have different approaches to their work. For example, J.P. Morgan and Morgan Stanley perform excellent credit research, so I am fairly confident with their ratings. These companies use their credit research information for their own book, so I can be assured that they are not selling an unattractive bond. Other reliable sources exist, which simply broadens the scope of opinions.

Question: What effect will monetary union have on the development of ABS?

Laternser: It will be a prime catalyst for these kinds of instruments because the EMU will be an incredible source of competition and will pressure market participants to operate efficiently. Protective country borders will no longer exist. Banks will respond to declining profit margins by securitizing parts of their balance sheets, such as credit card receivables or mortgages. This scenario will propel the growth of the ABS market. Without the EMU, some banks will find ABS an interesting alternative source of funding, but the need and pressure will not exist. I believe the popularity of structured products will grow and the EMU will be a strong catalyst to the development of the ABS market.

Appendix: Foreign Exchange Symbols Used

ATS = Austrian schilling
BEF = Belgian franc
CAD = Canadian dollar
CHF = Swiss franc
DEM = German mark
FRF = French franc
GBP = British pound
ITL = Italian lira
JPY = Japanese yen
NLG = Netherlands (Dutch) guilder
PHP = Philippine peso
SEK = Swedish krona
USD = U.S. dollar

Reference List

Adler, M., and B. Dumas. 1983. "International Portfolio Choice and Corporation Finance: A Synthesis." *Journal of Finance* (June).

Adler, M., and B. Prasad. 1992. "On Universal Currency Hedges." *Journal of Financial and Quantitative Analysis* (February).

Bekaert, G., and R.J. Hodrick. 1992. "Characterizing Predictable Components in Excess Returns on Equity and Foreign Exchange Markets." *Journal of Finance* (June).

Bilson, John F.O. 1981. "The 'Speculative Efficiency' Hypothesis." *Journal of Business* (vol. 54, no. 3).

———. 1984. "Purchasing Power Parity as a Trading Strategy." *Journal of Finance* (July).

Black, F. 1990. "Equilibrium Exchange Rate Hedging." *Journal of Finance* (July).

Cumby, Robert E. 1993. "Forecasting Exchange Rates and Relative Prices with the Hamburger Standard: Is What You Want What You Get with McParity?" Mimeo, Stern School of Business.

Dacorogna, M.M., U.A. Müller, C. Jost, O.V. Pictet, R.B. Olsen, and J.R. Ward. 1995. "Heterogeneous Real-Time Trading Strategies in the Foreign Exchange Market." *European Journal of Finance* (vol. 1, pp. 383–403).

Eichengreen, Barry, Andrew Rose, and Charles Wyplosz. 1996. "Contagious Currency Crises: First Tests." *Scandinavian Journal of Economics* (vol. 98, no. 4).

Ferson, W.E., and C.R. Harvey. 1994. "Sources of Risk and Expected Returns in Global Equity Markets." *Journal of Banking and Finance* (September).

Frankel, Jeffery. 1989. "Flexible Exchange Rates: Experience Versus Theory." *Journal of Portfolio Management* (Winter).

Froot, K.A. 1993. "Currency Hedging over Long Horizons." National Bureau of Economic Research Working Paper 4355.

Froot, Kenneth A., and Kenneth Rogoff. 1995. "Perspectives on PPP and the Long-Run Real Exchange Rate." In *Handbook of International Economics*. Edited by Gene M. Grossman and Kenneth Rogoff. New York: Elsevier Science.

Froot, Kenneth A., Michael Kim, and Kenneth Rogoff. 1995. "The Law of One Price over 700 Years." National Bureau of Economic Research Working Paper 5132.

Gastineau, Gary L. 1995. "The Currency Hedging Decision: A Search for Synthesis in Asset Allocation." *Financial Analysts Journal* (May/June).

Glen, J., and P. Jorion. 1993. "Currency Hedging for International Portfolios." *Journal of Finance* (December).

Guillaume, D.M., M.M. Dacorogna, R.D. Davé, U.A. Müller, R.B. Olsen, and O.V. Pictet. 1994. "From the Bird's Eye to the Microscope: A Survey of New Stylized Facts of the Intradaily Foreign Exchange Markets." Olsen & Associates Internal Document DMG.1994-04-06.

Harvey, C.R. 1991. "The World Price of Covariance Risk." *Journal of Finance* (March).

Jorion, P. 1985. "International Portfolio Diversification with Estimation Risk." *Journal of Business* (July).

———. 1989. "Asset Allocation with Hedged and Unhedged Foreign Stocks and Bonds." *Journal of Portfolio Management* (Summer).

———. 1994. "Mean–Variance Analysis of Currency Overlays." *Financial Analysts Journal* (May/June).

Kaminsky, Graciela L., and Karen K. Lewis. 1996. "Does Foreign Exchange Intervention Signal Future Monetary Policy?" *Journal of Monetary Economics* (April).

Karnosky, Dennis, and Brian Singer. 1994. *Global Asset Management and Performance Attribution*. Charlottesville, VA: Research Foundation of the Institute of Chartered Financial Analysts.

Krugman, Paul. 1979. "A Model of Balance-of-Payments Crises." *Journal of Money, Credit and Banking* (vol. 11, no. 3).

———. 1993. "Recent Thinking about Exchange Rate Determination and Policy." In *The Exchange Rate, International Trade and the Balance of Payments*. Edited by Adrian Blundell-Wignall. Sydney: Reserve Bank of Australia.

Levich, R.M., and L.R. Thomas. 1993a. "The Merits of Active Currency Risk Management: Evidence from International Bond Portfolios." *Financial Analysts Journal* (September/October).

———. 1993b. "Internationally Diversified Bond Portfolios: The Merit of Active Currency Risk Management." National Bureau of Economic Research Working Paper 4340.

Lewis, Karen K. 1995. "Occasional Interventions to Target Rates." *American Economic Review* (September).

Mark, Nelson C. 1995. "Exchange Rates and Fundamentals: Evidence of Long-Horizon Predictability." *American Economic Review* (March).

McBeth, J.D., and D.C. Emmanuel. 1993. "Tactical Asset Allocation: Pros and Cons." *Financial Analysts Journal* (November/December).

Meese, Richard A., and Kenneth Rogoff. 1983. "Empirical Exchange Rate Models of the Seventies: Do They Fit out of Sample?" *Journal of International Economics* (February).

Michaud, R.O. 1989. "The Markowitz Optimization Enigma: Is 'Optimized' Optimal?" *Financial Analysts Journal* (January/February).

Nesbitt, S.L. 1991. "Currency Hedging Rules for Plan Sponsors." *Financial Analysts Journal* (March/April).

Perold, A., and E. Schulman. 1988. "The Free Lunch in Currency Hedging: Implications for Investment Policies and Performance Standards." *Financial Analysts Journal* (May/June).

Pictet, O.V., M.M. Dacorogna, U.A. Müller, R.B. Olsen, and J.R. Ward. 1992. "Real-Time Trading Models for Foreign Exchange Rates." *Neural Network World* (vol. 2, no. 6).

Roll, Richard. 1979. "Violations of Purchasing Power Parity and Their Implications for Efficient International Commodity Markets." In *International Finance and Trade*. Edited by Marshall Sarnat and Giorgio P. Szego. Cambridge, MA: Ballinger.

Rosenberg, Michael. 1993. "Currency Forecasting: Theory and Practice." Merrill Lynch & Company International Fixed-Income Research.

———. 1996. *Currency Forecasting: A Guide to Fundamental and Technical Models of Exchange Rate Determination*. Chicago: Irwin.

Sachs, Jeffrey D., Aaron Tornell, and Andres Velasco. 1996. "Financial Crises in Emerging Markets: The Lessons from 1995." *Brookings Papers on Economic Acitivity.*

Solnik, B. 1974. "An Equilibrium Model of the International Capital Market." *Journal of Economic Theory* (July/August).

———. 1993a. "Currency Hedging and Siegel's Paradox: On Black's Universal Hedging Rule." *Review of International Economics* (June).

———. 1993b. "The Performance of International Asset Allocation Using Conditioning Information." *Journal of Empirical Finance* (March).

———. 1993c. *Predictable Time-Varying Components of International Asset Returns*. Charlottesville, VA: Research Foundation of the Institute of Chartered Financial Analysts.

———. 1996. *International Investments*, 3rd ed. Reading, MA: Addison–Wesley.

Throop, Adrian W. 1993. "A Generalized Uncovered Interest Rate Parity Model of Exchange Rates." Federal Reserve Bank of San Francisco *Economic Review* (vol. 3, no. 2).

Self-Evaluation Questions

1. Which of the following can help avoid a speculative currency crisis in emerging-market currencies?
   - I. Willingness on the part of government to raise interest rates.
   - II. Sufficient foreign reserves.
   - III. Willingness on the part of government to increase the government's debt burden as a percentage of GDP.
   - IV. Ability to increase government spending as a percentage of GDP.

   a. I and IV.
   b. II and III.
   c. II and IV.
   d. I and II.

2. According to Willner, which of the following fundamental changes in market dynamics have altered the behavior of currency returns and currency risks?
   a. More favorable secular economic trends.
   b. Better central bank and government policies.
   c. Ease of capital mobility around the globe.
   d. All of the above.

3. Except for the United States and Japan, for any home currency, the majority of fixed-income and equity investments lie outside the home country.
   a. True.
   b. False.

4. According to Lundin, which of the following best characterizes hedging foreign currency risk?
   - I. If we want to optimize portfolio value at risk, a hedge ratio of –1 is optimal.
   - II. If the correlation between the underlying investment and foreign exchange equals zero, foreign exchange may provide further portfolio diversification.
   - III. The optimal hedge ratio depends on the investment time horizon and percentage of a portfolio allocated to foreign assets.
   - IV. Managing currency exposure is unavoidable for investors with less than 5–10 percent of a portfolio allocated overseas.

   a. I and II.
   b. II and IV.
   c. II and III.
   d. III, and IV.

5. Kritzman points out that the relevant correlation is between currency returns and the foreign-asset returns denominated in the base currency.
   a. True.
   b. False.

6. In comparison with constrained mean–variance analysis, mean–variance tracking-error optimization almost always produces which of the following?
   a. Higher expected returns with a lower standard deviation of returns.
   b. Higher standard deviation of returns at the same level of expected return and tracking error.
   c. Lower tracking error at the same level of expected return and standard deviation.
   d. Higher expected return with lower tracking error and lower standard deviation of returns.

7. According to Kritzman, which of the following option strategies best protects a portfolio from currency losses beyond a specified threshold *only* when the portfolio's local return simultaneously falls below a prespecified hurdle value?
   a. A zero-premium put spread collar.
   b. A hybrid collar.
   c. A contingent currency option.
   d. A down-and-out barrier put option.

8. Which of the following accurately describes the pricing behavior of a contingent currency option?
   a. Decreasing portfolio volatility increases the value of the contingent option.
   b. Decreasing the correlation between the currency return and the portfolio return increases the value of the contingent option.
   c. Decreasing the hurdle value on the portfolio sharply decreases the option value.
   d. All of the above.

9. Which of the following is the major problem with using the variance ratio to enhance currency returns?
   a. Unknown forward volatility.
   b. Period-specific problems with capturing trends.
   c. Lack of data.
   d. The variance ratio is a valuable and accurate active-management tool.

10. According to Day, over the 1978-97 period, data show that when the forward premium has been ________, and when foreign interest rates have been ________ than domestic interest rates, currency returns have been ________?
    a. Positive, higher, and negative.
    b. Positive, lower, and negative.
    c. Negative, lower, and positive.
    d. Negative, lower, and negative.

11. Which of the following statements best describe currency overlay management?
    I. An overlay manager is not permitted to increase pre-existing exposure by the net purchase of foreign currency.
    II. Currency overlay allows international asset allocation to expand safely and rapidly.
    III. Currency overlay adds value by reducing risk and increasing return.
    IV. A currency overlay manager operates in conjunction with the underlying portfolio managers to improve communication.
    a. I and IV.
    b. II, III, and IV.
    c. I, II, and III.
    d. II and IV.

12. Layard-Liesching lists which of the following as the main difference(s) between forecast-based and risk-controlling philosophies of currency management?
    a. Forecast-based approaches offer substantially higher returns than risk-controlling approaches.
    b. Forecast-based approaches have substantially negative interim outcomes compared with risk-controlling approaches.
    c. Forecast-based approaches focus on enhancing returns using market timing, while risk-controlling styles focus on risk reduction.
    d. All of the above.

13. Which of the following best describes currency risk?
    a. Over the very long run, the interest rate differential corrects exchange rate movements.
    b. Over the short run, currency makes a greater impact on stock returns than on bond returns.
    c. Over the short run, currency makes no impact on stock returns.
    d. Currency risk and local market risk are additive.

14. The supply of and demand for currency affect exchange rates and the size of the currency risk premium.
    a. True.
    b. False.

15. According to Solnik, tactical currency allocation is based on the observation that currency risk premiums and expected returns fluctuate over time.
    a. True.
    b. False.

16. Stannard identifies which of the following as the most important goal in a performance attribution analysis?
    a. Pinpointing the strengths and weaknesses of the portfolio manager.
    b. Determining the value added through active management.
    c. Presenting results in a manner consistent with the decision-making process.
    d. Decomposing results into those attributable to asset allocation and those attributable to security selection.

17. Which of the following statements best describes the currency effect?
    I. The forward premium effect is often regarded as a form of allocation effect.
    II. The forward premium effect is the consequence of interest rate differentials between countries and the portfolio being over- or underweight in a particular market.
    III. The management of currency movements in excess of those predicted by forward premiums is measured in the currency management effect.
    IV. Expected exchange rate changes, accounted for by differential interest rates, can be hedged away.

a. I and IV.
b. II and IV.
c. I, II, and III.
d. All of the above.

18. According to Laternser, with the advent of European monetary unity, which of the following risks will become the most important risk for fixed-income analysts?
    a. Instrument risk.
    b. Country risk.
    c. Collateral risk.
    d. Credit risk.

19. According to Laternser, which of the following best describes fixed-income investing in the post-EMU era?
    I. Investors will diversify vertically into lower quality credits and horizontally into emerging market sovereign risk.
    II. Because of the size of the new euro debt market, its liquidity will be better than the U.S. Treasury market.
    III. The EMU will promote the development of a European structured product market.
    IV. Based on initial credit ratings, government bond yields will be lower than interest rate swap yields.
    a. I and II.
    b. III and IV.
    c. I and IV.
    d. I and III.

Self-Evaluation Answers

1. d. Willner explains that a balance-of-payments-crisis model—which uses key variables such as government economic policy, the trade balance, and foreign currency reserves—is useful in identifying potential emerging-market currency crises. Sufficient currency reserves, a willingness on the part of government to raise interest rates, and the character to impose politically unpopular austerity measures can successfully stave off a currency crisis.

2. d. In addition, our ability to analyze currency movements has improved. Advances in technology, not only computing technology but also analytical technology, now include cointegration, variance ratios, error correction, and generalized autoregressive conditional heteroscedasticity (GARCH) models.

3. b. Lundin notes that although Japan and the United States account for a large fraction of fixed-income (30.1 percent and 27.2 percent, respectively) and equity (23.1 percent and 42.6 percent, respectively) investment opportunities, no one country has a majority.

4. c. To optimize portfolio value at risk, a hedge ratio of –1 is not necessarily optimal. If the correlation between the underlying investment and foreign exchange equals zero, then foreign exchange may provide further diversification and no hedge is recommended. The optimal hedge ratio depends on the investment time horizon and the percentage of the portfolio allocated to foreign assets. Managing currency exposure is unavoidable for investors with more than 5–10 percent of a portfolio allocated to nondomestic assets.

5. a. Although currency returns may have low or negative correlation with local foreign-asset returns, the relevant correlation is between currency returns and the foreign-asset returns denominated in the base currency. For example, a U.S. investor should not care about the correlation between the yen and the local return on Japanese stocks but should care about the correlation between the dollar-denominated return of Japanese stocks and the yen currency returns.

6. c. Kritzman explains that mean–variance tracking-error optimization increases expected return with the same level of standard deviation and tracking error, reduces standard deviation of returns at the same level of return and tracking error, or produces less tracking error at the same level of expected return and standard deviation.

7. c. Contingent currency options protect a portfolio from currency losses beyond a specified threshold only when the portfolio's local return simultaneously falls below a specified hurdle value; they cost less than traditional currency options but also provide less protection.

8. c. According to Kritzman, higher portfolio volatility raises the value of the contingent option because it increases the likelihood that the option will end up in the money. Decreasing the correlation between the currency return and the portfolio return reduces the value of the contingent option. As the correlation goes down, portfolio returns and currency returns are less likely to decline at the same time. Decreasing the hurdle value on the portfolio, quite sharply decreases the option value.

9. b. According to Day, the variance ratio is a useful first step to analyzing potential currency trends. It helps identify parameters for assessing the time scale of trends, but it has period-specific problems with capturing trends.

10. b. Data show that when the forward premium has been positive (negative) and when foreign interest rates have been lower (higher) than domestic interest rates, currency returns have been negative (positive). This finding suggests that active management of currency can enhance portfolio returns.

11. c. Layard-Liesching states that, once appointed, a currency overlay manager operates with total independence from the underlying international equity or bond managers. All the currency overlay manager needs to know is the currency allocation of the underlying managers and the instruments they hold.

12. d.

13. a. For most currencies, over the very long run, the interest rate differential corrects exchange rate movements, according to Solnik. In the short run, currency makes a large contribution to bond returns because bond market risk is smaller than equity market risk and because the correlation between interest rate and currency movements is positive. In the short run, currency makes a significant, but marginal, contribution to stock returns. This contribution is lower for a diversified portfolio than for a single foreign market or currency. Currency risk and local market risk are not additive. For example, the variance in the Swiss franc is equal to the local market variance (e.g., in Italian lira) plus the foreign exchange variance plus 2 times the correlation of the two multiplied by the standard deviation of each source of risk: the local market risk of the Italian lira stock and the Swiss franc/Italian lira exchange rate risk.

14. a. Solnik observes that the supply of and demand for currency affect exchange rates and the size of the currency-risk premium. Thus, currency prices adjust because of supply and demand factors—influencing the currency risk premium—until the new equilibrium exchange rate is determined. The interest rate differential is basically a risk premium that net foreign investors are willing to pay to hedge their currency risk and to induce domestic investors to provide the vehicle for that hedge.

15. a. Although the currency market is an efficient market with somewhat predictable risk premiums and expected returns, the efficient market hypothesis never states that expected returns should be constant over time. Expected returns fluctuate because of such factors as business cycles, changes in the market environment, and individuals' relative degree of risk aversion. So, the risk premium can fluctuate over time. Central banks are important players in the currency markets, and empirical evidence indicates that they are consistent losers because their objective function is to stabilize the market. Thus, opportunities exist for tactical currency allocation to add value.

16. c. Performance attribution analyzes a portfolio manager's success in the context of the investment decision-making process. Regardless of the algorithms used, the most important goal in a performance attribution analysis is to present the results in a form that is consistent with the decision-making process. It is also a valuable business management tool for portfolio managers, highlighting the strengths and weaknesses in the investment process and identifying evidence of continuing skill. Performance attribution decomposes excess portfolio returns into three components: the asset allocation effect, security selection effect, and currency effect.

17. c. According to Stannard, expected exchange rate changes, accounted for by differential interest rates, cannot be hedged away because the pricing of forward currency contracts assumes that such expected currency changes will happen. This relative interest rate impact is measured in the forward premium effect.

18. d. With the advent of the EMU, credit analysis will be the paramount issue in European fixed-income research—especially because EMU participants will relinquish the right to issue debt in their own currencies. Vertical and horizontal diversification will also make credit risk the focal point for fixed-income analysis.

19. d. Although a huge overall euro market—a market much bigger than the U.S. Treasury market—will develop, the liquidity of the euro market may not be as great as many investors think. The overall market size, about USD3.5 trillion, will not drive bid–ask spreads, but the relative size of each tranche and selective issues will. No component of the euro market is bigger than the U.S. Treasury market, a fact that may have a surprising impact on liquidity. An interesting implication of initial credit ratings is that interest rate swaps could trade through some government bond yields. If credit risk for a given government is rising, interest rate swaps, which have a better credit rating than the respective government bonds, could trade at a lower yield.

Selected Publications

AIMR

AIMR Performance Presentation Standards Handbook, 2nd edition, 1997

The Consumer Staples Industry, 1996

Deregulation of the Electric Utility Industry, 1997

Economic Analysis for Investment Professionals, 1997

Finding Reality in Reported Earnings, 1997
Jan R. Squires, CFA, *Editor*

Global Equity Investing, 1996

Global Portfolio Management, 1996
Jan R. Squires, CFA, *Editor*

Implementing Global Equity Strategy: Spotlight on Asia, 1997

Investing in Small-Cap and Microcap Securities, 1997

Investing Worldwide VIII: Developments in Global Portfolio Management, 1997

Managing Endowment and Foundation Funds, 1996

Managing Investment Firms: People and Culture, 1996
Jan R. Squires, CFA, *Editor*

The Media Industry, 1996

Risk Management, 1996

Standards of Practice Casebook, 1996

Standards of Practice Handbook, 7th edition, 1996

Research Foundation

Company Performance and Measures of Value Added
by Pamela P. Peterson, CFA, and David R. Peterson

Currency Management: Concepts and Practices
by Roger G. Clarke and Mark P. Kritzman, CFA

Economic Foundations of Capital Market Returns
by Brian D. Singer, CFA, and Kevin Terhaar, CFA

Emerging Stock Markets: Risk, Return, and Performance
by Christopher B. Barry, John W. Peavy III, CFA, and Mauricio Rodriguez

Initial Dividends and Implications for Investors
by James W. Wansley, CFA, William R. Lane, CFA, and Phillip R. Daves

Interest Rate and Currency Swaps: A Tutorial
by Keith C. Brown, CFA, and Donald J. Smith

Interest Rate Modeling and the Risk Premiums in Interest Rate Swaps
Robert Brooks, CFA

Sales-Driven Franchise Value
Martin L. Leibowitz